THE LEGACY OF LEADERSHIP

How One Generation of Leaders Influence Another

Dr. D. Robert Kennedy

Copyright © 2019 Dr. D. Robert Kennedy

All rights reserved. No part of this publication may be reproduced, stored in a retrieved system, or transmitted, in any form or by any means, electronic, mechanical, photocopying, recording, or otherwise, without the prior written permission of the publisher.

Printed in the United States of America.

ISBN:978-1-7321890-8-9

Publisher: Legacy Seminars
         11503 Belvidere Road
         Bowie, MD 20721

About the Author

Dr. D. Robert Kennedy is the pastor of the Emmanuel Worship Center in Alexandria, Virginia, a congregation of the Allegheny East Conference of Seventh-day Adventist. He has been in leadership practice, as a pastor, Conference/Union Departmental Director, College/University professor and administrator for 48 years. He has traveled all the continents and many islands, of the world, preaching, teaching and offering seminars in leadership in the church and non-profit organizations, and along with his wife who holds a doctorate in Urban Education, in family life leadership and education. Together they have three sons, three beautiful daughters in law, and seven wonderful grandchildren, with whom they are always interfacing about legacy.

In this collection of opinion editorials and two sermonic notes, Dr. Kennedy has given attention to issues in the legacy of leadership, with the hope that his reflections can motivate those who read to be more effective in their circle of influence.

DEDICATION

To my dad, Robert Kennedy, who was nearly at the age of biblical patriarchs 105 years, and mom, Mary Kennedy, who passed away when she was 96 years old. In my book, they have left all of us children a powerful legacy of leadership, that is replicated in only a few families in our world, today. We are still asking ourselves, with much praise to God, how has it happened, that they have ten children who are ordained church elders, effective community and organization leaders. None of us wish to boast, but truth be told, our parents legacy of leadership is something that cannot be taken lightly. Dad and Mom have never claimed to be perfect, but, at their worst, they did their best, and placed all of us in the hands of God, who has given to us the influence that we continue to share in our families and communities.

This is one of the chairs that was made by our father and given to each of his children. Some grandchildren already have one of the chairs and they appreciate it as an indication of the legacy of leadership that Robert Kennedy has left for future generations.

Table of Contents

Introduction 1
The Legacy Of Leadership 3
Your Actions In Leadership 6
Your Vision Of Leadership 8
Your Values In Leadership 10
Your Boldness In Leadership 13
Your Initiative In Leadership 17
Your Character In Leadership 19
Your Courage In Leadership 22
Your Leadership Decisions 25
Your Communication In Leadership 28
Your Judgment In Leadership 30
Caring About Others In Leadership 33
Facing Criticism In Leadership 35
Finish What You Start 38
Your Authenticity In Leadership 40
Creating Your Leadership Climate 43
Checking Your Leadership Culture 45
Your Courtesy In Leadership 47
Winning Is [Not] Everything 50
Be Careful How You Judge In Leadership 52
Your Knowledge In Leadership 55

Giving And Receiving Gifts In Leadership 57
Building Bridges In Leadership 59
Leading With Authenticity 62
Money And Morality In Leadership 65
Leading With Authority 67
Sexual Discretion In Leadership 69
Speaking The Truth In Leadership 72
Leading With Determination 75
Leading In A Time Of Crisis 78
Leading With Responsibility 80
Leading From The Past 82
Leading In The Present 84
Leading To The Future 86
Leading With Confidence 89
Putting People Down 92
Building Other People Up 94
Leading With Integrity 97
Valuing Spirituality In Leadership 99
Showing Strength In Leadership 102
The Compassion Factor In Leadership 105
The Faith Factor In Leadership 108
The Grace Factor In Leadership 111
Taking Advise When You Lead 113
Taking The Fire When You Lead 116
The Charisma Of Leadership 118
The Dignity Of Leadership 121
The Corrupting Influence Of Leadership 123

The Cost Of Leadership	126
Assessing How You Lead	129
The Greatest Temptations Of Leadership	132
The Credibility Of Leadership	135
The Effectiveness Of Leadership	138
The Accountability Of Leadership	141
Leading In The Age Of New Media	144
The Celebration Of Leadership	149
Making A Difference In Leadership	152
Parenting And The Legacy Of Leadership	169
The Making Of Leaders For The Next Generation	186
Conclusion	204
Appendix	206

INTRODUCTION

Since 2009, I have been writing opinion columns for the Local Talk Newspaper in Newark, New Jersey, and reflected on many themes, sometimes following a topic for a whole year. After a year of reflecting on issues in leadership, I have been encouraged to collect the reflections and share them at a time when we seem to be facing one of the greatest crisis in public leadership that we have ever encountered in our world. Here in the United States, it is being noted that some individuals believe that to present themselves as bold leaders, they need to show bluster.

In the view of a host of persons, this attitude or style, is diminishing what constitutes effective leadership. It seems, today, like everybody has something to say about leadership - whether to understand it, practice it, criticize it, challenge it, or to focus on its effectiveness. After listening to all that is being said, you might be wondering what more can be said to focus on the legacy of leadership for today.

My view in these reflections is that although much has been said, much more needs to be said, because every age creates more complex issues for leadership. When I think today, of the most significant needs of leadership, I think of Josiah Gilbert Holland's poem and its appropriateness for today. It reads:

> GOD, give us men! A time like this demands
> Strong minds, great hearts, true faith, and ready hands;

Men whom the lust of office does not kill;
Men whom the spoils of office cannot buy;
Men who possess opinions and a will;
Men who have honor; men who will not lie;
Men who can stand before a demagogue
And damn his treacherous flatteries without winking!
Tall men, sun-crowned, who live above the fog
In public duty, and in private thinking;
For while the rabble, with their thumb-worn creeds,
Their large professions and their little deeds,
Mingle in selfish strife, lo! Freedom weeps,
Wrong rules the land and waiting Justice sleeps.

Whether we such among our men or women, we need leaders who can understand that their influence counts and that they leave a mark upon the everlasting world.

THE LEGACY OF LEADERSHIP

Life is about legacy. Leadership is about legacy. Wherever we walk we leave a legacy. When we talk we leave a legacy. Whatever we do we create a legacy. In elementary school, I was taught a song from the poetry of Henry Wadsworth Longfellow. It goes like this:

> I shot an arrow into the air,
> It fell to earth; I knew not where;
> For, so swiftly it flew, the sight
> Could not follow it in its flight.
> I breathed a song into the air,
> It fell to earth; I knew not where;
> For who has sight so keen and strong,
> That it can follow the flight of song?
> Long, long afterward, in an oak
> I found the arrow, still unbroken;
> And the song, from beginning to end,
> I found again in the heart of a friend.

Yes, life is about legacy. If more of us thought of our legacy, we would be more careful about what we say, what we do, and how we live.

When I think of Abraham Lincoln and Adolf Hitler, I see two men – one who sought to unite a nation, while the other divided a nation. One man showed dignity and respect for all humanity while the other hatred and vengefulness. I also think of King David of Israel who tried to unite his nation and of his grandson Rehoboam who divided the nation.

I could cite many more leaders who sought to build unity and others who created hatred and division. However, my point is to challenge us to ask ourselves and our contemporary leaders about the kind of legacy that is being left in our nation. And to the rest of us, what legacy might we leave in the organizations, communities, homes, and families that each of us will seek to lead? What kind of legacy are we leaving? We all need to ponder carefully, the following questions that will help us to determine the sort of legacy we are leaving.

1. How much are we concerned about opening and leaving doors open for others?
2. How much are we interested in building up others?
3. How much are we interested in creating gratifying relationships with others?
4. How much are we interested in building a culture of love, instead of hatred?
5. Are we always aware of how our decisions of today will impact the next generation?

When the Apostle Paul came to his final days he offered up this valedictory recorded in 2 Timothy 4: 6-8 (NKJV):

> For I am already being poured out as a drink offering, and the time of my departure is at hand. 7 I have fought the good fight, I have finished the race, I have kept the faith. 8 Finally,

there is laid up for me the crown of righteousness, which the Lord, the righteous Judge, will give to me on that Day, and not to me only but also to all who have loved His appearing.

Much could be said on this valedictory, but the one thing I observe is the sense of satisfaction that the Apostle felt. He felt good about his legacy and his future. How is your legacy?

YOUR ACTIONS IN LEADERSHIP

As I listened to the question posed to a presidential candidate as to when he would start acting more presidential, my mind was directed back to the 16th century famed Italian writer, Machiavelli, who wrote The Prince. This book is considered one of Machiavelli's shortest books but it has had the most significant impact on the world, even until today. It is accepted to be a profound analysis of the political culture of the time, with exciting suggestions as to how rulers might secure and sustain their power and honor. Some ideas point to the virtues and others to the vices that should be used as a guide for obtaining and maintaining control. In effect, whatever works should be used. The chapters - Conquest by virtue, Conquest by fortune, and Conquest by criminal value - fascinated me because they all conclude that whatever it takes to win and to rule is to be used.

Yes, I am convinced that at this time in our current presidential campaign, the Machiavellian political philosophy is being tested. I cannot say this will follow the campaign, and those using it will win; but, it is of interest that it is being tested. And there seems to be a public that is accepting it without much criticism. Some people are thinking that it is good for entertainment, but to such, I would say that fiction often becomes reality. It is assumed that people seek what they value. Even though there are those who say that they do not like what they are seeing and hearing, but will hold their noses and vote for to secure a win, they need to be careful because they might have accepted unwittingly, a philosophy that they know is against their heart value.

Yes, I am watching with a prayer and hoping that those who are campaigning would be reading and following better books than The Prince. I am hoping that the varied publics across the land will be able to say that Machiavellianism is not acceptable because such will be a poison to the American political system.

And for those of us who lead outside the political culture, I suggest that it is time we take stock of the ways we seek to obtain leadership and how we try to sustain it. Here are some questions which we must ponder carefully.

1. Are we seeking to play a game between virtue and vice?
2. Are we clear about the respect we offer each other?
3. Do we accept decency, dignity, and discipline as non-negotiable principles of leadership?
4. Are we consistent in the way we seek leadership, and how we sustain it?
5. Or do we play the game between vice and virtue?

Again, I conclude this reflection with a prayer. I ask the Lord to help us lead a life above the Machiavellian standards because leadership is not only for the short term. Leadership impacts a culture over time. In this I pray, Lord help me never to think that Machiavelli wrote a textbook for me. Help me to turn to your word, because I can find in it all the principles I need to make me presidential or in any other portfolio.

YOUR VISION OF LEADERSHIP

I left college "many moons ago," but I still remember what one of my renown professors used to say, "A man that lacks vision, needs supervision." After repeating what he considered his excellent idea, he would pause to see what we thought because he also knew he sounded truly profound and Scriptural. Proverbs 29:18 (King James Version) reads, "Where there is no vision, the people perish."

There is no need to test the idea, for it is proven again and again that successful families, homes, churches, schools, institutions, companies, communities, other organizations, and nations are all led by persons of vision. As is said, vision is an essential component for success because it defines what one would do with one's life, if he/she has unlimited time, resources, information, and staff. If a leader wants to succeed, such a leader must do more than strive to survive. Such a leader must have a vision and make a significant commitment to the fulfillment of the vision.

If there is a crisis in leadership today, it is a crisis of vision. Many individuals think that a vision is any little projection of the mind on the humanistic realm. But one commentator on Proverbs 29:18 states, "The vision is the actual contact between God and the human spirit, which is the necessary condition of any direct revelation." If one is not in contact with God, one might have what is called a vision, but it will be a bad vision.

When I think of a leader who had contact with God, I often think of Moses. While he was tending his father-in-law's sheep on the backside of Mount Sinai, he had a vision of God in the burning bush. (Cf. Exodus 3:1-17). The vision was so compelling that he became fearful, but God was merciful to him and opened his eyes to what was demanded. God worked with Moses and promised to go with him if he would keep to the vision before him. Moses accepted the commission contained in the vision and went to Egypt where he shared it with the leaders of Israel, who helped him to make it known to the people of Israel. Moses also confronted Pharaoh with the vision, and Pharaoh was forced to allow Moses and the people of Israel to leave Egypt.

In biblical and secular history, Moses is known as one of the world's greatest leaders. He was as effective as his vision. His vision was the energy behind his effort. It helped him push through the problems that he faced with Pharaoh and with his people in Egypt. By the vision he inspired the leaders of Israel to unite and gather the people to leave Egypt, thus fulfilling what was said at the start, that with a vision much will be accomplished. A visionless leader will become frustrated by achieving little. A person with a vision will find strength from inner convictions, while a visionless person finds strength from external conditions. A person with a vision continues when problems arise while a visionless person quits when the road becomes difficult.

Do you live by a vision? If not, why not? If you intend to live a useful life, I invite you to pray to God for a vision. To be a visionary, you need time to think, meditate, pray, read, and study God's word.

YOUR VALUES IN LEADERSHIP

How might one's personal beliefs and values impact one's capacity to lead or work in any organization? I have noted how the question is being asked, in varied ways, to members of the FBI. They have been brought before the United States Congress to defend their activities in the institution. And I am fascinated, for it seems that those asking the question are not considering how much their beliefs and values are coloring their questioning. I wish I could help them to see their biases, but I leave that for another day.

The point is that it is very much the case that organizations are most affected by the personal values of those who lead and participate in them. I was quite amazed when a president of one of the organizations in which I worked came to my office and asked whether or not his personal beliefs and values were judged so long as he was fulfilling the administration of his office. I felt it quite strange that he should have asked me, but I had to tell him the truth. It is hard to separate one's personal beliefs and values from how one leads or what one does. Individuals who have tried to do so, have often admitted the contradictions; they try to live with the double biography, but it does not work, because it makes them feel like hypocrites.

Let me ask you as a reader of this reflection to contemplate the following list of questions.

- What do you believe in?
- What is your most profound conviction?
- To what are you fundamentally committed?
- What would you die for?
- What can you do without compromising your integrity?
- What do you value?

Would your response be: Wealth? Power? Pleasure? Fame? Self-indulgence? Material possessions? Pride? Covetousness? Revenge?

Or, put in a positive frame, would it be: Generosity? Justice? Humility? Peace? Respect? Self-control? Forgiveness? Compassion? Character?

It is good to make a check on yourself/ourselves at times, for too many individuals do not know what they believe or value at their core. This is why they cannot stand up for what is right. They dally and settle for anything that they feel will give them an advantage or make them win. If they lead an organization, they will let anything go until the organization is destroyed.

I genuinely admire the Prophet, Daniel. In the Bible it is said of him, "But Daniel purposed in his heart that he would not defile himself with the portion of the king's meat, nor with the wine which he drank: therefore, he requested of the prince of the eunuchs that he might not defile himself." (Daniel 1:8 NKJV).

Do I need to say more? I think not, because we all know the destruction created in the world by people who lack a definite sense of values.

YOUR BOLDNESS IN LEADERSHIP

Various qualities make for effective leadership. However, among the most significant is the quality called bold leadership. Someone might argue that if bold is just a little four letter word, why is it so dominant? The answer lies in the fact that multiple studies of leadership success over time have proven that the only time when the effective transformation takes place in any organization or community is when a leader takes the helm with boldness. We are not to diminish the other significant qualities of leadership, but the present context of life seems to elevate boldness to a high point, especially because many persons are confusing courage with bluster.

Let us give some attention to boldness here. People describe leaders as bold because such leaders see opportunities or challenges and act courageously to solve them. They argue that a courageous leader:

- Never settles for the status quo. They always see or seek out opportunities.
- Is unable to let a needed change go unaddressed.
- Will walk head-on into both positive and negative stress situations and conquer them.
- Stays to see the results of their work.
- Is positive – with moments of self-doubt that they push through and never let their teams suffer.
- Makes very (hard) strategic decisions about where and how they invest.

- Relies on top talents with whom they might choose to surround themselves.
- Is team-oriented. They are "we" people interested in success broadly, not selfishly.
- Anchors their decisions in what is right for the customer. We have yet to find a successful bold leader who is not customer-centric.
- Often feels lonely within their organization. They are acutely aware of the changing burden that others do not see or fully understand.
- Is not always effective. The successful ones know when, how much, and how to recruit others and build momentum toward their goals.

Among the most impressive of the biblical characters that expressed boldness, from my perspective, is the great Jewish reformer, Nehemiah. According to the biblical record, he was the cupbearer of King Artaxerxes. That means, he was the most trusted assistant of the king. Nehemiah had to taste any food prepared for the king before he would partake of that which was placed before him. Nehemiah did it to make sure that Artaxerxes would be preserved should anyone seek to poison him. Of course, Nehemiah, in spite of the importance of his job, was not permitted to walk into the king's presence without an invitation and particular permission.

However, after Nehemiah inquired about the condition of his people and his brother reported to him that all was not great back home in Jerusalem, Nehemiah was troubled. The walls of Jerusalem were in disrepair. Enemy groups were trying to overrun the land. The faith of the people had been corrupted. The leaders were oppressing the people. The families were falling apart through mixed marriages. The people were conflicted with one another, in their struggle for survival. After listening to the report, Nehemiah became very sad and began to pray. Nehemiah did not only pray but without an appointment, he went in to see the king. When the king saw him, the king asked what the problem was? Why was his countenance so sad? Nehemiah explained and requested permission to go and visit Jerusalem to see what he could do to resolve the issues. Nehemiah was given the authority he sought, and he went.

Nehemiah had many moments in which his boldness was challenged. For example:

1. When he secured letters to give him safe passage and went up to Jerusalem, he did not meet with the leaders but went by night to survey the conditions. It seems at times that he was by himself.
2. Having surveyed the city and noting the circumstances, he called for a meeting with the leaders to seek their cooperation and outline the tasks for repairing the wall.
3. After receiving their pledge for cooperation, he put them to work.
4. Sandballot, Geshem and Tobia and their cohorts ridiculed the work.
5. But Nehemiah never got discomfited. He only challenged them back.

6. When the people complained of how they were being oppressed by the rulers, Nehemiah called for a meeting with the rulers and rebuked their injustices.
7. Nehemiah's boldness was so significant that the Jewish rulers backed down from what they were doing to oppress the people. The reform was so powerful that even some of the heathen joined to eat at Nehemiah's table.
8. There are many other moments in which Nehemiah's boldness was challenged, but sufficient is said here to help us argue that the work that was set forth was effectively completed.

In effect, Nehemiah was incredibly bold. He was courageous and courteous. He was determinedly faithful and full of courage. He took risks. He had the qualities of a true reformer and knew how to balance boldness with benevolence, passion with compassion, and justice with love. He was not brash. He was not a bully. He became angry but used that anger to resolve the problems of the people positively.

As we have noted, the lessons in Nehemiah's life of leadership are multiple. We will revisit his boldness in future reflections, but sufficient is said here to make the point that Nehemiah's audacity was positive, not negative. He held to his dignity and integrity. He never used harsh words, labeled people, or project on them. He put himself on the line, and lived a model of morality before God, before the king, before his people and before the people beyond his borders. No one needs wonder why Nehemiah was able to achieve so effectively what he had set forth to do.

YOUR INITIATIVE IN LEADERSHIP

As a follow up to our discussion on the significance of boldness in the life of leaders, we think of the importance of taking the initiative. That says great leaders are not successful by just sitting around and waiting for things to happen to them, or around them, but they take the initiative that makes things happen. In my kind of work, it makes no sense to wait to be directed, I have had to move. I have had to be creative. Such is how things happen.

I do not know how successful your life has been without initiative, but let me encourage that if ever things have happened without your action, you would be much more effective if you took action. Let me suggest six areas in which you might wish to take the initiative as you explore your life's direction.

1. How about taking the initiative to make some new friends? Don't sit around and wait for people to come to you; find them, for lots of people are longing for relationships and do not know how to open up to them. You can help them.
2. How about daring to do something to change a bad habit and, or improve a good habit. Remember that habits form character.
3. How about turning your ideas into actions? You might have some great ideas, but they are not worth anything until they translate into action.

4. How about taking the initiative to lay out an investment strategy? I am not a financial advisor, but I like to encourage people in this area because too many persons wait on others to do what they can do for themselves.
5. How about helping to initiate a transformative social agenda. Do not just sit around and allow the politicians and the media to do things the way that you might not like. Get involved.
6. How about initiating a new level of relationship with God? I cannot speak for everyone, but this is what I know, that quite often we are left feeling distant from God. We don't feel His presence. We feel like we are drifting apart. Or maybe we feel like we were never connected with Him at all. It is not God who has left us, but often we are so busy doing our own thing, that we have left Him. So my encouragement is that in this area too, we will seek to initiate a new relationship with Him.

Yes, thank God that life offers us opportunities to take the initiative. We do not have to live on a plane of regrets recounting our failures. We can begin again. We can change. Even God promises to begin again. In the book of Revelation, it is recorded, "I will make all things new." In seeing what mess we have made for ourselves, God will not allow us to live as we are. He will make everything new. It is an excellent motivation for me to begin again. How is it for you?

YOUR CHARACTER IN LEADERSHIP

In the public culture of our day, it seems evident that leadership is not anymore being defined by good personal character, but by charisma, power, popularity, possessions and emotional connections. The view expressed seems to be true concerning the leadership of many countries of the day and is indubitably true concerning the current presidency of the United States. While some persons are calling out the president for what they call the lack of good character, there seems to be a core of supporters who think that a good character does not matter. They do not seem to be much concerned about integrity, ethics, morality, judgment, self-awareness, wisdom, compassion, justice, emotional health, and the other good qualities that are admired in leaders for many years. But are accepting of qualities that are the manifestation of bad character? Of course, it might be offered that the loss of focus on character leadership is not only in the public sphere but also in the private realm. For example, it is noted that within many religious communities, leaders with evil characters, are left in positions of authority after they have betrayed their offices. Many leaders are chosen, not because of their excellent personal character, but because of their looks, popularity and other things that have nothing to do with character or leadership.

In offering the above critique, I do not just wish to be sardonic, but to make the critical point that we need to seek out individuals with good characters in our contemporary world, as it was in the past, where the moral character was highly valued. As is said, there was a time when people would not allow individuals without good characters in public offices. When they sought for leaders, they found those qualities of character that could be admired and emulated.

In the biblical frame, when the Apostles in the Early Christian Church looked for deacons to help them lead, they asked for individuals of good character. Here is what is said in the selection of the first deacons; "Then the twelve summoned the multitude of the disciples and said, 'It is not desirable that we should leave the word of God and serve tables. Therefore, brethren, seek out from among you seven men of good reputation, full of the Holy Spirit and wisdom, whom we may appoint over this business. . .'" (Acts 6:2-3).

Yes, effective leaders lead with strong, personal and moral character. They are unwavering, trustworthy, and principled. They are not easily persuaded, dissuaded or distracted. They work from conviction instead of convenience. They will not "cut corners" to win. They will not lie to succeed. They will not take drugs or cheat. Character leaders are courageous leaders. They have staying power in everything that they do.

A summative point is that character is not something that one develops over-night. Here is how Ralph Waldo Emerson states it, "Sow a thought and you reap an action; sow an act[ion], and you reap a habit; sow a habit, and you reap a character; sow a character, and you reap a destiny." Indeed, a positive character does not come to a person in the quick of a moment. It is something that one must seek to develop. One has to work hard at it. One must discipline oneself to obtain it. But once one achieves it, one will be able to fight the temptations that may come to destroy it. How is your character? What have you been doing to make sure it develops in a positive way? Don't forget that the greatest temptations of a leader are:

- The temptation to self-trust
- The temptation to control power
- The temptation to focus on prestige
- The temptation to ignore how a leader can influence the culture of an organization
- The temptation not to take care of one's health
- The temptation to generalize thinking and strategies.
- The temptation to lose patience and become discouraged.
- Living up to the false hopes of others.

Have you been able to overcome the temptations?

YOUR COURAGE IN LEADERSHIP

In face of the ongoing political discourse, with candidates trying to outdo and outtalk one another, I have decided to continue my discussion on leadership that makes a positive difference. My present reflection today rests on one word I have heard again and again - COURAGE. Professor Paul Tillich, who taught at Union Theological Seminary many years ago before my attendance there, I focused on this word in his book *The Courage to Be* (oneself). In his effort to clarify the existentialist philosophical point of view, he noted the significance of the word connecting it to themes such as courage and fortitude, courage and wisdom, courage and self-affirmation, and courage and anxiety, etc. Of course, the two subsections in the book that grabbed my attention were "Absolute faith and the courage to be," and "The courage to be as the key to being itself." Sue Patton Thoele's book, *The Courage to Be Yourself: A Woman's Guide to Emotional Strength and Self-Esteem,* provides the necessary tools to help readers transform their fears into the courage to express their authentic selves. Of course, her book might be considered a spin-off from Tillich's book. Whatever it is, it is quite obvious that COURAGE is a most necessary ingredient for all of life and leadership. The Scottish poet and novelist, Robert Louis Stevenson is reported to have said, "Everyday courage has few witnesses. But yours is no less noble because no drum beats for you and no crowds shout your name." In effect, every day of our lives we need courage; not just for the momentous events but also more often as we make decisions or respond to circumstances around us.

Think of it, when Moses stood with Israel before the Red Sea, being hemmed in by a mountain on the right and another on the left, with the advancing Egyptian army behind them, and the Israelites panicking; at the divine command Moses told Aaron to lift his rod, then commanded the Israelites to go through the Sea. It took courage, but all were safe on the other side while Pharaoh and his army drowned in the Sea. All through the wilderness travel, in victory after victory, there was the exercise of COURAGE. And after 40 years when Moses was about to depart this life, in handing over the leadership to Joshua, he placed a great emphasis on the word. He said, "Be strong and be of good courage." *(Deuteronomy 31:6; Joshua 1:9)*.

Yes, COURAGE. Courage to:

>Stand up and be counted
>Stand up for principle
>Make the right choices and decisions
>Speak for the voiceless
>Yes, COURAGE. Courage not to:
>Allow yourself to panic
>Be subjected to crowd mentality
>Be driven by the polls
>Compromise your values
>Be cast down by ridicule
>Dilute your belief in God

We need COURAGE. Courage to say" Yes" and "No" when we need to.

Yes, the courage to be true to God, to ourselves and others. It is said that:

- Leadership is inspiring others towards a common purpose
- Leadership is building a spirited team
- Leadership is creating an environment that promotes innovation
- Leadership is sharing power and information
- Leadership is sharing tasks and holding those with whom we share accountable
- Leadership is putting joy and celebration in the accomplishments of people
- Leadership is about finding the source of confidence required to help others
- Leadership is going about to improve other people's abilities

Yes, this kind of leadership is courageous leadership.

YOUR LEADERSHIP DECISIONS

This week, in my pursuit of bold leadership, I note the significance of decision-making. Here is one area in which many individuals make a failure of their lives. They do not know how or when to make decisions. Life drifts along around them. Circumstances drive them; they float along, going anywhere the waves will toss them. After such attitude, they become frustrated and blame the world for their failures.

Yes, what I am saying is that making effective decisions is profoundly essential if one desires to be a leader that makes a significant difference in history. The fact is, decisions do matter, and leaders need to learn how to make them. Decisions are most often weighty, and one who understands the consequences of making them might feel overwhelmed, at times, whenever one has to make them. But making decisions, one must, as far as we are told, understand that "procrastination is the thief of time." Therefore, if a person does not wish to gamble his/her time away, then such a person needs to learn that decisions are made with precision.

There are rules to follow in effective decision-making. Here are a few that I highlight that might be helpful to you.

1. Be thoughtful - Thoughtful reflection is constructive, but do not just think, act.

2. Do not be driven by pressure- If you allow public (or peer) pressure to inspire you, you will often make the wrong decision. Always waiting on consensus to make decisions is a demonstration that one lacks the capacity for effective decision-making.
3. Be careful of impulsivity - Learning not to jump to conclusions
4. Take time for consultation - Remember that your decisions might not involve you alone; think of how each decision might affect your family. Talk to your family, friends, mentors, and advisors. They can be helpful, but ultimately remember the choice is yours to make.
5. Get the appropriate information and knowledge about a subject before you make a decision - But do not slow down your decision by just seeking information. At times, you need to make a decision regardless of the lack of total knowledge.
6. Faith and Trust - Remember that you have to decide by taking what knowledge you have to go forward.
7. Learning to pray - There is a lot of power in prayer when one needs to make a decision. I believe that Jesus was the most effective example of how prayer impacts decision. I do not have a place here to tell how prayer works, but I can tell you that it works when I have to make decisions.
8. Scriptural consultation - The Bible has the counsel of God, and if you want to bring God into your decision, you need to listen to what he says. You might not be brought up to the

mountain like Moses to hear what God says, but you can read what God said to him and get the right direction.

Yes, if you are going to be a productive person, especially as a leader, you need to learn how to make decisions.

YOUR COMMUNICATION IN LEADERSHIP

After one of my many marriage-counseling sessions, I could not stop thinking of the theme on which I am reflecting today, namely "Connection and Communication." Whenever people come to me contending that their greatest challenge is a lack of effective communication, I can, most often, since their lack of connection.

Effective communication demands connection. By connection I do not just mean what is on Facebook, Snapchat, Snappish, LinkedIn, Twitter, Email, Texting or other means provided by the Web. That is good, and sometimes profoundly beneficial and transformational to any social climate and culture. But anyone who carefully assesses these means of connection will admit that they have their downsides; they cannot replace the personal presence or other ways of being intimately connected.

Connection is about personal presence, friendly sharing, personal knowledge, warmth, responsiveness, personal emotion, trust building, caring, showing concern, creating a climate of understanding, respect, love, transparency, and vulnerability. Watch any couple that has all of these in the mix of their relationship and see how they communicate. Those who come to me and are so connected, have never raised communication as a number one issue. It is true that these couples might not say that they have been successful in every attempt of their conversation, but find it easier to resolve a communication-based conflict because they have a connection.

Let me use this reflection also to reference the varied leaders I observe who understand the significance of connection. They always seem more effective in the kind of leadership they give, whether it is in the home, the school, the church or public sphere. Whenever one is connected, one will be able to communicate more effectively.

In contemplating what is stated above, I often think of the prayer life of Jesus that revealed a profound connection between Himself and his Father. Check these prayers in the following Bible passages:

> *And Jesus lifted up His eyes and said, "Father, I thank You that You have heard Me. And I know that You always hear Me, but because of the people who are standing by I said this, that they may believe that You sent Me."- John 11:41-42.*
>
> *And He was withdrawn from them about a stone's throw, and He knelt down and prayed, saying, "Father, if it is Your will, take this cup away from Me; nevertheless, not My will, but Yours, be done." Then an angel appeared to Him from heaven, strengthening Him. - Luke 22:41-43.*

What do you think? Did you sense the intimacy of connection? Let me assure you that even if you are not connected as Jesus and His Father were, if you have a fraction of their relationship, your communication would be much more effective.

YOUR JUDGMENT IN LEADERSHIP

I have known the proverb "Do not [just] judge a book by its cover" for a long time, but two incidents and a general situation that happened lately have caused me to re-focus on the proverb. The one incident happened when I went to Barnes and Nobles to browse through a few books, as is my custom before making a purchase. After perusing a few books, I picked up one with a rather interesting title. I read the blurbs, and the preface and they sparked my interest to explore further. I leafed through a couple of pages and was shocked at what I saw. It was nothing but "dirt" and a stark contrast to the cover information. In utter dismay, I quickly returned the book to the shelf, because I knew it was not intended for me.

Another incident happened when I went to a Christian bookstore and bought a book with an exciting title. The back cover summary told how a mother dealt with grief after her son was killed in a car accident. The mother was the author, and that heightened my urge to read it. But soon as I started, I began to take note that several chapters contained views that were alien to my understanding of death and the resurrection. I shared the book with my wife without telling her about my findings. I wanted her to tell me what she thought about the content. As soon as she started to read she began to complain concerning the contradictions, she felt with the biblical view of the teachings I named above. Eventually, she called up the bookstore manager and asked the manager whether they had vetted the book before placing it on their shelf.

My general observation is connected to the presidential election process. Those individuals involved are using their best charms. As competitors, they make every effort to show how their judgment and trust quotient are much more consistent than those who are opposing them. One audacious young man at a Democratic Town Hall asked Secretary Clinton how does she react to the fact that his "friends" see her as "dishonest." In answering his question, Secretary Clinton did not seek to defend herself, but instead, noted that this was the culture of politics, today. She stated that this is what was done to her and her husband for over 40 years. The news media has been giving slanderous profiles of them. The suggestion is "Do not [just] judge a book by its cover."

In several ways, the proverb is suitable for all of us. It encourages us to take time to read what is on the inside of books. In regards to human life a biblical text that I have been quoting in several Op/Eds state, "Do not consider his appearance or his height, for I have rejected him. The LORD does not look at the things people look at. People look at the outward appearance, but the LORD looks at the heart." (1 Samuel 16:7). This is quite instructive for all who have an interest in the political leadership or leadership in different spheres of life, "Do not [just] judge a book by its cover."

Do not just look at titles, read carefully what is on the inside. Do not only make sure a story is one of interest. Make sure you find out what is at the depth of the story. Be careful of deceptions, because deceptions are often so deeply embedded that they are sometimes tough to be identified. Seek what is genuine. Do not just pay attention to so-called public reputation; search out for what is inside a character.

CARING ABOUT OTHERS IN LEADERSHIP

How many of us as leaders are genuinely concerned about others? The question has been pressed upon me as I continue to reflect upon this arduous ongoing presidential election cycle. I have heard candidates talking about their concern. But it is concern about their party rules and actions. They are concerned when they claim that they are being disfavored. However, when they speak of their opponents, they seem not to have any concern about the name-calling, smears, and put-downs that they are using. They do not seem concerned about their tone or/and characterizations that they use to destroy their so-called competitors. They do not seem to care whether they hurt, demean, or embarrass the ones over whom they are seeking to win.

Maybe I should not be making these suggestions or raising any questions as a pastor, here, because I need to understand that the game of politics is played differently than what one might expect in churches. The values are different. The standards are different. The expectations are different. But are we to accept that there is so significant a difference when what is done has a profound impact on our children and families? It is quite unfortunate that often the values and standards found in the churches run parallel to what is taking place in the public culture. The churches are expected to be different, but are they?

My interest, of course, is not to compare institutions, but to challenge everyone who calls himself/herself a leader, whether in the public sphere or the private spaces of church or home. It should be understood that we cannot be effective if all we do is spend time name-calling, putting down, hurting, demeaning, disrespecting, or embarrassing one another. When I do marriage counseling and have to focus on communication, I help couples to see that their words, tone, attitude, and actions matter in how they show concern for each other. The same is to be said for the way we relate in private or public contexts of politics and so on.

Let us not forget that, those with whom we relate are humans; they have personalities, feelings, mentality, dignity, hope, and passions, which can be hurt. Not that they are to expect that in this world, all is going to be nice and comfortable, but we need to be cautious because whatever we do to others, it will be done back to us; not just as an aspect of divine judgment, but in our present relations.

The Bible says, "Anyone who does wrong will be repaid for their wrongs, and there is no favoritism." (Colossians 3:25 NIV). "Give, and it will be given to you. Good measure pressed down, shaken together, running over, will be put into your lap. For with the measure you use it will be measured back to you." (Luke 6:38 ESV).

Ask yourself, frankly, "Do you have a genuine concern for others?"

FACING CRITICISM IN LEADERSHIP

The other day I heard a short comment on my car radio about the fact that one of the presidential candidates was being attacked from all sides. What was of interest, to me, was the follow-up instruction, namely, that if the candidate would be wise, the candidate should continue to focus attention on the direction where the candidate wished to go, and not to give notice to all of the attackers. The commentator said, "You can't keep your eyes in the rearview mirror, all the time if you hope to drive ahead."

When I heard it, I said that is solid instruction; considering that leadership, whether in the public political culture or other contexts, seem to be always open to criticism. If one is of the personality type that easily gets irritated, frustrated and angered, one will find that any criticism will draw them away from their purpose.

In reality, a leader needs to be aware that criticism is a part of the trade of leadership. Somebody says, "If you cannot take the heat, get out of the kitchen." This is not to say that one needs to commend those who spend their time, digging up dirt and trying to pile it on those about them who lead. But it is a reality that there are persons in our world, who live by the laws of negativism. They will always find reasons to engage in that which is negative and destructive. They want to bring down those about them, who they think are their competitors. They want to make sure that no one is left standing but them, and, maybe, those who they believe are just like them.

However, one who understands the culture of criticism will know that one is never to be distracted by it. One needs to learn how to respond and grow from criticism. In effect, we should never allow criticism to lead us away from our goal.

In his appeal to the Christian Communities that were facing criticism and persecution in his time, the Apostle Peter wrote the following words that can be quite instructive to any leader who leads today:

> Dear friends, do not be surprised at the fiery ordeal that has come on you to test you, as though something strange was happening to you. But rejoice since you participate in the sufferings of Christ, so that you may be overjoyed when his glory is revealed. If you are insulted because of the name of Christ, you are blessed, for the Spirit of glory and God rests on you. If you suffer, it should not be as a murderer or thief or any other kind of criminal, or even as a meddler.
>
> However, if you suffer as a Christian, do not be ashamed, but praise God that you bear that name. - 1 Peter 4:12-16 NIV.

Think about Peter's words and see how they can help you to face criticism. No matter how effective you are in creating a vision some people will:

- Fight you
- Oppose you
- Criticize you

- Seek to put obstacles in your way

When everybody else is pointing to obstacles, true leaders look for solutions. Do you know the way to find solutions? If you do not know, just ask God to help you.

FINISH WHAT YOU START

When I come to the end of a year, I usually evaluate to see whether I have accomplished all the things that I had set forth to do at the beginning of the year. When in my review, I find that I accomplished that which I set forth to do, I get excited. I feel satisfied and of course, successful. On the contrary, when I have not finished what was intended I feel frustrated. I am a rather determined person and like to know that I finish what I have started. Consequently, whenever I do not finish that which I intended, I ask myself "Why?"

For my attitude to task completion, I express profound gratitude to my parents for the foundation they laid and their insistence on my finishing a task, as I grew. At times when the assigned tasks were not done to their satisfaction, they called me back. As they pointed to the unfinished task, I often wondered what they meant; soon I learned that task completion was critical.

Yes, we are finishing another year, and I believe that, like me, many of you are taking some time to evaluate what you had set forth to do. How do you feel about what you have accomplished this year? I hope you feel satisfied. In John 17:4 Jesus was praying to his Father when he said, "I have brought you glory on earth by finishing the work you gave me to do." Jesus felt good. Finishing what he came to earth to do was not easy. He faced the greatest of temptations in the wilderness to give up on his mission. He had much opposition from the religious leaders who did not like his effort to reform their broken system. Even his disciples, who could not understand what he was doing, tried to distract him, but he persisted to the point of completion. From the cross, in his final breath, he cried out, "It is finished." The work that he had come to do was completed.

He left his work as a powerful example as to how we are to go about our lives. We need to learn that the lives we live are not going to be effective until we finish what God intends for us to do. At the end of his life, the Apostle Paul said, "I have fought the good fight, I have finished the race, I have kept the faith. Finally, there is laid up for me the crown of righteousness, which the Lord, the righteous Judge, will give to me on that Day, and not to me only but also to all who have loved His appearing." (2 Timothy 4:7,8 NKJV).

The most significant point that we need to remember in the finishing of any task is that not only are we evaluating ourselves but that God is evaluating or judging us. He has given each of us a mission on earth. He has set forth expectations for each of our lives. If we have done what we need to do, not only will we feel satisfied in ourselves, but heaven will endorse what we have done; and one of these days, the King of kings will say to those on His right hand, "Come, you blessed of My Father, inherit the kingdom prepared for you from the foundation of the world." (Matthew 25:34 NKJV).

If what we are doing is what God wants us to do, let us try to finish it, because finishing will bring us the greatest joy we can have in the paradise of God.

YOUR AUTHENTICITY IN LEADERSHIP

In listening to one of the presidential debates a few nights ago, I could not help but taking note of one candidate calling out another about being "disingenuous." It forced me to ask myself, "Who among all those running and hoping to win their positions are going to be genuine at this time?" I did not ask the question to indict anyone or to offer a pass to the one who was called out or the one who was calling out the other; but I asked it, because, from what I have been seeing or hearing, there seems to be a lack of genuineness throughout the entire political culture. It is of interest to me that people are willing to accept disingenuousness with a cheer as if such is acceptable, and that one is only called out when it is against the desired outcome.

It is also amazing to me how a crowd will shout at a presidential candidate who is waving a Bible at rallies, while the waver seems to have no real knowledge of the Bible. It appears that the Bible is only being used to whip up the crowd and cause a shout. Maybe such individuals should read the Bible carefully as it rightly assesses the problem that there is a manifestation of deception and wickedness in our times that makes it difficult for people to hear the truth. The Apostle Paul says it best; "For this reason, God will send upon them a deluding influence so that they will believe what is false, so that they all may be judged who did not believe the truth, but took pleasure in wickedness."

(2Thessalonians 2:10-12). The fact, as I see it, is that disingenuousness does not only rest with the political candidates but with everyone who is willing to accept the lies.

My point is that genuine leadership is much needed today because we need a profound transformation in our culture. So we need to challenge ourselves and our leaders to stop the phoniness and become genuine leaders. Let us stop nurturing the falsehoods and instead, encourage authentic leadership that will have respect for the truth. Such guidance should understand that the devil is ready to take over people's minds, confuse them and destroy them. And we who call ourselves leaders should not allow this. We need to be doing all that is necessary to preserve the mission and high values that will help us to protect our world, local organizations, and communities.

In the ongoing election cycle, it is good to ask, "How does a leader behave under the pressure to win?" The question should not be only focused on those who are campaigning, but each of us needs to ask this of ourselves when we participate in the competitive games of life. Can we turn on and off our genuine button as we please? Are we communicating positive messages to others that adhere? It is said, "To be genuine, one must be one's self under all conditions, situations, and circumstances." How are we in our homes? How are we in our churches? How are we in our schools? Or any community in which we are being called to lead? It is also said, "There is never a place for phoniness, pretense, or falsehood." In our leadership and followership, we need to make sure that we keep the focus on being true. A verse I learned in school, "You must be true to yourself if you the truth will teach. It takes an overflowing heart to give the lips full speech," aptly summarizes my point on genuine leadership.

We should never allow the desire to win to lead us into falsehood. Let us be genuine and authentic.

CREATING YOUR LEADERSHIP CLIMATE

Many persons who are reading this reflection might think that the only kind of climate that one needs to talk about is that which connects to Global Warming. However, as our election season heats up, it is necessary that we give some attention to the kind of climate it is creating. As we assess the present climate, it is clear that a lot is changing, and such has the potential to affect succeeding generations.

Some persons might not wish to assess the changing social climate, but I offer that it might be wise to take a second look at the quakes, storms, and erosions that are affecting our ecosystem. Climate changes are occurring that are destroying our national culture and organizational systems. Ask a variety of individuals about how they feel concerning the present conditions and they will tell you, it is hot, cold or lukewarm. Ask the angry crowd how they feel, and they will tell you it is chilly and cold.

Whatever the judgments might be, it is essential that each of us face the following questions:

1. Are conditions being created to build unity and community?
2. Are the seeds of anger being sown to perpetuate hatred and conflicts?
3. Are there opportunities for hope and peace?

Yes, the climate in which we live is important, not just as it concerns our ecosystem, but as it concerns our social system. And it seems to me that as leaders, we are responsible to create a pleasant climate in which people can live. Political leaders need to ask, "How is our political climate?" Economists need to ask, "How is our economic climate?" Responsible parents need to ask, "How is the climate of our homes? Are our homes habitable for our children?" Teachers need to ask, "How is the school climate? Is it wholesome for learning?" Church leaders need to ask, "How is the climate of our churches? Are they healthy for faith development?"

We read in the Bible of a church that did not know its climate condition and the Lord offered a rather severe judgment against it thus:

> So then, because you are lukewarm and neither cold nor hot, I will vomit you out of My mouth. Because you say, 'I am rich, have become wealthy, and have need of nothing'—and do not know that you are wretched, miserable, poor, blind, and naked— Revelation 3:16, 17 NKJV).

As we reflect on the climatic conditions being created, let us ponder these two questions: How might God be judging the climate of the context in which I am? What am I contributing to the health of the climate?

CHECKING YOUR LEADERSHIP CULTURE

One significant interest of leaders who make a difference in organizations is to focus on the culture of their organizations. Serious leaders try to understand the culture of the organization at the moment they pursue leadership. They endeavor to find what are the negatives within the culture and seek to transform it in positive ways.

It is more than unfortunate that in the current political climate there is a radical degradation of our culture. What was thought as being the high values of our American life is eroding. It seems, at times, that only a few, a very few people, are taking note and being accountable in seeking to transform the culture in positive ways.

I am getting frustrated that even some of us who name ourselves Christians are reflecting the most negative aspects of our culture. To such, I need offer this reminder as Jesus told his disciples, that whatever the culture of the world, it was not to be so with them (Cf. Matthew 20:26; Mark 10:43). The world's use of authority, power, and values, was to be different in the organization among his disciples.

The Apostle Paul said the same when he reminded the Christians in Roman "Don't let the world around you squeeze you into its own mold, but let God re-mould *(sic)* your minds from within, so that you may prove in practice that the plan of God for you is good, meets all his demands and moves towards the goal of true maturity." (Romans 12:2, Phillips)

A quote from Kurt Vonnegut that commonly circulates on the Internet says, "Be soft. Do not let the world make you hard. Do not let the pain make you hate. Do not let the bitterness steal your sweetness. Take pride that even though the rest of the world may disagree, you still believe it to be a beautiful place."

In face of what I see happening in the prevailing culture, let me use my pastoral office to encourage anyone who is reading this reflection. Do not let the world corrupt you, or harden your heart, making you violent, bitter, resentful, hateful or steal away your sweetness. Take time to make peace. Find time to create joy. Work for cooperation with those about you. Seek to overcome the rancor.

Not everyone might be a public leader, but all of us who live in our private spaces have the power of influencing others. We need to acknowledge the negatives that we see. We need not just spend time blaming others for them. Wherever we are, we need to contribute to positive change. Let us build a better culture.

YOUR COURTESY IN LEADERSHIP

I cannot forget one of the most profound little gems I learned when I was just a Tot. It says, "Always say please when you ask for anything and thank you when you get it." It still serves me well and has been a benefit in my relationships at home and in the public sphere where I lead. All human beings appreciate these courtesies, and I do welcome when they give them back to me. For all the kindnesses done to me by others, I certainly have much for which to be thankful. And for all the blessings that God has offered to me, I genuinely need to praise.

What I have concluded as I go through life is that much more of my time need to be dedicated to thanksgiving, for the kindness of others and the blessings of God come to me every day. It is true that people are not always kind, but I have decided that their actions will not determine whether I am to say thanks. In fact, I have found that, sometimes, adverse actions give me an opportunity to test my attitude, so I say thanks.

The point I am seeking to make is that for all my wisdom to make great decisions, and for all my ability to do strategic thinking and accomplish any task, I am still imperfect in many ways and need to praise God for his mercy and his grace in giving me success.

Let me take the reason for thankfulness outside of my sphere into public life where our leaders are working hard to keep us safe. As I have learned, there are 16 intelligence agencies across our land here in the United States that are working to keep us safe. They have a lot of confidence in what they are doing. They are working overtime. However, they know that they are vulnerable. So while they are dependent on their technical skills and wisdom, they need also to understand that true safety rightly reposes in the God we serve. He is the one who gives us provision and protection. Like the prophet Jeremiah says:

> *Through* the Lord's mercies, we are not consumed,
> Because His compassions fail not.
> *They are* new every morning;
> Great *is* Your faithfulness! (Lamentations 3:22, 23 NKJV).

In effect, my encouragement to us all is that we take some time to be thankful. It is a benefit in all relationships and in fact it has been proven that a life lived with thankfulness is much more productive for the individual and those around. Let us not do it because of its utility, but because we recognize that we are ever blessed with the mercies from all the relationships that we have been given.

- "I believe the greatest legacy a leader can leave is having developed other leaders." - John Maxwell,
- As a leader, you can't develop others until you improve yourself.
- Leadership is having values to share. Values are caught not taught

- Leadership is not a position; it is how people affect other people and make a difference in their lives
- Leadership is setting an example
- Leadership is articulating strategies for the future
- Do not be hasty in word or impulsive in thought to bring up a matter in the presence of God. For God is in heaven and you are on the earth; therefore, let your words be few.
- If you are always preoccupied, you will not be a visionary
- Loss of faith in what God wants us to do
- Loss of a sense of history – what God has done in the past
- Loss of the promise - What God is seeking to do in the future
- Loss of perspective – Loss of what God is doing in the present
- They say, "I can do all things through Christ who strengthens me." – Philippians 4:13
- The Lord desires to develop leaders in his church for these last days of earth's history
- Acts 2:17
- "'In the last days, God says, I will pour out my Spirit on all people. Your sons and daughters will prophesy, your young men will see visions, your old men will dream dreams

WINNING IS [NOT] EVERYTHING

An idea that placed before the nation during a past presidential race was that "winning is everything;" but is it. As I have given attention to the process, the creative tactics being used to win amazes me. I have seen the projection of utopian dreams, the media manipulation, the character assassinations, the name calling and labeling, the fear-mongering, the waving of Bibles, and all kinds of other of gimmicks that I have been wondering where is the seriousness. The idea is that "It is all about winning." But, what happens after winning? Is there a strategy for governing?

The above questions have led me to reflect on one part of a story I reviewed this morning in my devotional. In Judges chapters 7 and 8, we are told of how Gideon came into prominence from one of the smallest clans in Israel and how he led Israel into battle against the Midianites with only 300 soldiers. After his signal victory, he returned home where the community invited him to become ruler over them. Here is how it is stated in chapter 8:22-27:

> Then the men of Israel said to Gideon, "Rule over us, both you and your son, and your grandson also; for you have delivered us from the hand of Midian." But Gideon said to them, "I will not rule over you, nor shall my son rule over you; the Lord shall rule over you." Then Gideon said to them, "I would like to request you, that each of you would give me the earrings from his plunder." For they had golden earrings because they *were* Ishmaelites. So they answered,

"We will gladly give *them.*" And they spread out a garment, and each man threw into it the earrings from his plunder. Now the weight of the gold earrings that he requested was one thousand seven hundred *shekels* of gold, besides the crescent ornaments, pendants, and purple robes which *were* on the kings of Midian, and besides the chains that *were* around their camels' necks. Then Gideon made it into an ephod and set it up in his city, Ophrah. **And all Israel played the harlot with it there. It became a snare to Gideon and to his house**. (Emphasis mine).

Wow! What a tragedy? Gideon knew how to win, but did not know how to govern. He had some great qualities for governing such as being humble and generous, but he did not know or care to govern. He lacked the discipline that was necessary to take control and exercise authority, administer policy, make effective decisions, delegate responsibility, stabilize the society, and build unity. He was not able to stand up to the pressure from those who lobbied him to be like the very nation over which he had gained the victory. So, despite his great success in winning, he left a heritage of apostasy and lawlessness in Israel.

The point should be clear to all of us who are seeking to be leaders in whatever sphere we find ourselves-the home, church or public community- that winning is not all. We need to learn how to govern. We need to learn self-control. We need to make sure that in our influence and actions we create positive legacies. Any effective governing begins with self-government. So let each one of us, look at ourselves, first.

BE CAREFUL HOW YOU JUDGE IN LEADERSHIP

The untimely death of Judge Antonin Scalia caused much debate in the media and other public squares concerning the kind of contributions he made to the Supreme Court over his 30 years of service. There are also questions concerning the appropriate timing of his replacement and the power of the Presidency to make the appointment. I am not trying to enter this public debate, although there is a great temptation since I hear so much fallacy and disrespect with the political rancor that is undergirding much of the debate. For one thing, I wish that much more time was given to the Scalia's family to grieve their loss, instead of the immediate rancor concerning his replacement. Of course, the squabbling over his replacement might teach us, as leaders, how indispensable we are. No matter how much people tell us that we are important, we should not take them too seriously. It would be interesting if we could see how soon we are replaced after our death.

Yes, there is much discussion on a replacement for Antonin Scalia. Myriads of questions are being asked. What kind of judge do we need? Should it be a rabid constitutionalist or a radical conservative? Who will replace him? Who will pick the one to replace him? Should this President make the choice? Should the next President do it?

From a spiritual reflection, my interest is not so much what the public and the politicians are asking, but whether as a judge he practiced justice according to the standards of the divine. Here are a few Scriptures that should guide every judge and every leader.

> Judge not according to the appearance, but judge with righteous judgment -John 7:24.

> Do not pervert justice; do not show partiality to the poor or favoritism to the great, but judge your neighbor fairly - Leviticus 19:15.

> And I charged your judges at that time, "Hear the disputes between your people and judge fairly, whether the case is between two Israelites or between an Israelite and a foreigner residing among you - Deuteronomy 1:16.

> This is what the LORD Almighty said: 'Administer true justice; show mercy and compassion to one another - Zechariah 7:9.

> You judge by human standards; I pass judgment on no one - John 8:15.

> Have you not discriminated among yourselves and become judges with evil thoughts - (James 2:4)?

On reading and hearing these Scriptures, can we say that we have learned anything? Are the labels that we are affixing to the Justices sufficient to deal with the issues that are to be judged? Do we wish for favoritism when justice is done? Do we think of compassion when we judge? Are we affected by money when we judge? How do we judge? Not only must we think of justice about the public courts, but also in every position of leadership in which we are, we need to ask.

YOUR KNOWLEDGE IN LEADERSHIP

In listening to the bluster of some of the current political candidates I have been pressed to raise the question more and more as to what will make for a compelling difference in leadership. The answer that comes through to me at this time is **knowledge**. Unfortunately, many persons are giving most of their attention to the accumulation of information, but little to acquiring knowledge. In effect, many folks are giving heed to ignorance. Pardon my harsh evaluation, but it seems that on a historical basis, ignorance has led to a lot of personal destruction. This appears to be the reflection of the Bible. The passages below tell the story.

1. Part of Peter's Pentecostal sermon in Acts 3:17, reminding his hearers of what Israel and its leaders did concerning the crucifixion of Jesus. He said, "Yet now, brethren, I know that you did *it* in ignorance, as *also did* your rulers."
2. The message the prophet Hosea brought from God challenging Israel for their rejection of the laws, "My people are destroyed for lack of knowledge; because you have rejected knowledge." - Hosea 4:6,
3. The words of Jesus from the cross when he cried out, "Father, forgive them, for they do not know what they do." - Luke 23:34.

The issue being highlighted is that lack of knowledge is leading many to be ineffective in their lives and leadership. We have heard it said that much effort is being made to "dumb down" the society, and it appears real. Even though we are living in the information age, there seems to be a trend where a large part of our society seems to be getting more and more ignorant. I believe there are many reasons for the trend, including the fact that a large part of our community has stopped reading, researching, and thinking through issues. There seems to be those who are just following the crowd mentality.

This is why I wish to lay out a challenge to those who lead, so that we do not take advantage of people's ignorance, but that we seek to educate those about us as well as ourselves. Especially do I think it essential for those of us who lead in Christian organizations to make sure that we have the best of knowledge, and that those we lead are also encouraged to seek knowledge. Ignorance is a profound tragedy. And that is why it is rightly said, "If you think education is expensive, try ignorance."

It is true that knowledge can lead us to certain conceits. "Knowledge," says the Apostle Paul, "puffs up." (1 Corinthians 8:1). We have seen it all the time; people who think they know using it against those who lack knowledge. However, we cannot be afraid of knowledge. What is needed alongside of knowledge is the love and wisdom of God. We shall speak more about these in the future, but the point being made here is, if any of us want to make a powerful positive difference in leadership, we need knowledge. And of course, the best of knowledge that can be recommended is the knowledge of God. (Cf. Acts 17:11). It is often stated that the Bible is clear that the knowledge of God is the most valuable **knowledge** a human being can possess. The encouragement is that in all your search for knowledge; please seek the knowledge of God.

GIVING AND RECEIVING GIFTS IN LEADERSHIP

We are in a time of the year when the custom says that we are to give and receive gifts. The consumerist culture understands this and has been doing everything to heighten our desire for gifts. Our grandchildren have been preparing their gift lists since early October. They too are caught up in gifting.

Gary Chapman, a Marriage and Family Life consultant, author of the *Five Love Languages*, tells us that, among the five love languages is the giving and receiving of gifts. He argues:

- Gift giving is a fundamental expression of love that transcends cultural barriers.
- A gift is something that we can hold in our hands to indicate that we are being thought of.
- Gifts are visual symbols of love.
- Gifts come in all sizes and shapes.
- Gifts need not cost money, to be appreciated.
- If a person's love language is gifting, such a person will be moved emotionally by gifts.
- Sometimes one has to learn how to become a practical gift giver and receiver.
- One needs not wait for special occasions to give gifts.
- Gifts can be given at any time.

- The greatest gift is the gift of one's self - the gift of presence - physical presence in the time of crisis.

Of course, those of us who think of the gift of Christ will say to Chapman and all others, that Christ is the greatest gift that can be given; and the greatest that can be received. This, we know, is a big struggle in the world of religions where all do not accept or give the gift of Christ.

How do you relate to gifts? Are you one of those who likes to receive and never think of giving? Do you pause to think of how much time and care the givers take in selecting their gifts? At least one would hope that those who give gifts take the time to make the best selection. Do not just circulate the gifts that you got from the last year; take time to give the best gift you can. And for those of us who receive gifts, I also suggest that we take time to show our appreciation by saying thanks.

Now for those of us in positions of leadership, might I also present a caution regarding gifts? Might I suggest that we need to be careful about the gifts we give and the gifts we receive? Not everyone gives a gift with the pure motive of love. Gifts are sometimes given to impress. Therefore, if you as a leader give a gift, do not think that people owe you anything. Gifts are not to be thought of with a *quid pro quo* mentality. Do not seek to buy anyone with a gift. Do not allow yourself to be bought with a gift. Give your gift and receive your gift.

BUILDING BRIDGES IN LEADERSHIP

As political candidates try to position themselves, or as the media is scripting them, we can hear suggestions as to who is most aggressive or hawkish. Sometimes it seems they want it to appear that the most militaristic or hawkish will bring the highest security. I wish I could contend with them, for history has taught us that most often if ever, militarism does not always create safety and stability. War only leads to more and more conflict. When Jesus wished to speak of the cost of conflict, he said to his disciples, "Blessed *are* the peacemakers, for they shall be called sons of God" (Matthew 5:9). He understood it well that there is mutual benefit in peacemaking - "Blessed *are* the peacemakers," (Matthew 5:9 NKJV). Understood from the original, the peacemakers will share the joy of the peace they make. Those who make peace will find peace for themselves. The converse is also true that those who are ever creating conflict will live in misery.

Since my focus is on leadership, let me make clear that leaders who genuinely make a difference are those who will seek to create peace. Of course, we are told that peace begins in the heart. Miserable people try to make unhappy people. Contentious people attempt to develop controversial people. A great reality of life is that we can find individuals who seem to thrive on conflict in families, churches, local communities, and in the broader public sphere. Many such individuals are among our public leaders. In which case I must also question my role as a leader; "Am I a peacemaker or a conflict creator?"

For those who consider themselves leaders, as well as those who do not, I offer the following suggestions that might be helpful in making peace.

- Seek to understand others - The most significant reason for conflict is not being able to understand others.
- Respect goes a far way - Another reason for conflict is the disrespect that we have for each other.
- Watch your prejudices - At all points, our biases provide reasons for conflict
- Do not will yourselves to be so willing to introduce, and insist upon conflict to resolve issues. Does one need to resolve a dispute with a conflict? A lot of schoolyard bullies think so.
- Do not think it is a value to threaten and oppress others; There is no need to bully, belittle and shame others.
- Watch your words - Remember the proverb, "A word fitly spoken *is like* apples of gold in settings of silver" (Proverbs 25:11 NKJV).
- Be careful of falsehoods - Do not accept lies, they only get you angry, build hatred, and resentment.
- Pray for peace - While one Psalmist reminds his contemporaries to "Pray for the peace of Jerusalem" (Psalm 122:6), the prophet Jeremiah reminded his Jewish people in Babylonian exile to "seek the peace and prosperity of the city" in which they had to live (Jeremiah 29:7).

In effect, no family, community, organization, corporation, government or nation can effectively succeed without peace; so those who are leaders in them, need to promote peace. We need to learn how to speak the language of order rather than the language of war.

LEADING WITH AUTHENTICITY

Within the current election cycle, [of course, I am not sure if there are different cycles these days], I have heard the word "authenticity" being bantered about concerning certain presidential candidates. Authenticity seems to be profoundly powerful; it does affect how people think of leadership that can make a difference. The argument is that those who are most authentic are the ones that will receive the highest favorability and following. As you might expect, while I acknowledge the power of authenticity, I find it hard to agree with the reasoning that it is the truly authentic that are getting the favorability or the following. The case in point that brought me to think about authenticity and its impact on favorability and following was the boast of one candidate about his number one book. As he boasted, he asked, "Guess what my number one book is?" And he answered himself by saying "The Bible." Someone butted in, asking him to recite his most favorite Bible text. His response was, "I will not go there now." I do not know whether he has a favorite biblical text and can recite it, but I have noted that since that encounter, I have not heard again, that line of boast concerning his number one book.

Without giving too much credence to my illustration above, it is clear to me that the definitions and descriptions of authenticity, I hear in the news media, seem to be somewhat confusing. The word or idea is just being thrown about with the hope that the individual that the media anoints as authentic will be accepted, and the one the media indicts will be rejected. It is pathetic how often the media and the public in general, label pretenders as authentic, no wonder that the world has so many dictators and antichrists. People are looking to them and are getting fooled because they are being evaluated by their reputation rather than by their character, as God sees them. The media and a public that lack the wisdom of the divine create their reputation.

In doing this reflection, I am thinking of the biblical history, portrayed in the story of David and his selection as the king of Israel. The Lord told the prophet, Samuel, that he had rejected Saul as the king of Israel, and that he was sending him to Bethlehem to anoint the new king. Although Samuel was fearful that Saul might have killed him, he went to Bethlehem and met with the city elders who took him to Jesse's house for the anointing. Upon reaching Jesse's house, Samuel told Jesse about his mission; he had come to anoint one of his sons as king. Jesse, in response, called for his sons. As the first son Eliab, passed before Samuel, he that thought the Lord's anointed *was* before him. But the biblical text says, "But the Lord said to Samuel, 'Do not look at his appearance or his physical stature, because I have refused him. For *the Lord does* not *see* as man sees; for man looks at the outward appearance, but the Lord looks at the heart.'" Consequently, other sons of Jesse passed before Samuel, but he was not inspired to anoint them. After not receiving Divine approval to anoint any of those who came, Samuel inquired if there were another son. Jesse told him that there was one in the field tending the sheep. Samuel told Jesse to send for him. Immediately the young man from the field came and stood before Samuel, the

Lord said to Samuel, "Arise, anoint him; for this *is* the one!" We know today of David as the classical king of Israel. He had some faults, but it is said of him that he was a man "after God's own heart," because he was willing to do everything that God required of him. (Acts 13:22). In addition to his obedience, he was humble, faithful, repentant, respectful, reverent, trusting and devoted. These are not qualities that do not seem as important to the public and the media, but they are significant as we think of leadership that can indeed make a difference in the world.

MONEY AND MORALITY IN LEADERSHIP

The conviction of New York State Assembly Speaker, Sheldon Silver, on seven counts of influence-peddling seems to be within the norm of convictions for speakers of State houses these days. His conviction has not been put on the front pages of many newspapers or given much attention in the radio or TV news cycles, but the conviction needs not to be taken lightly. According to the report Mr. Silver has been involved in schemes by which he obtained nearly $4 million in exchange for using his position to help benefit a cancer researcher and two real estate developers.

Having reflected on Silver's multiple years of public service, I muttered to myself, "How tragic that he might spend the rest of his life in jail." Silver is 71 years old, and this scandal puts added strains and stress on his family; I feel for him and his family. Instead of leaving a legacy of dignity and respect for a generation of leaders that might have looked to him, his profile and likely epitaph are pathetic. Of course, only God knows what the end will be.

But my reason for mentioning Mr. Silver is to take note of the fact that the "Love of money," (1 Timothy 6:10) has been causing corrosion and perversion of a lot of individuals in public life today, and for too many ordinary individuals, as well. It seems to be an age-old problem. See what the brothers of Joseph did? They sold Joseph to Midianite traders for twenty shekels of silver. (Genesis 37:12-36). Also, note what Judas did? He sold Jesus for thirty pieces of silver. (Matthew 26:15; 27:3-10). Yes, the historical examples of money corruption are manifold. Ordinary persons and leaders, in all walks of life - secular and religious - have been cited for appalling and notorious deeds - all because of money. Yes! Money.

What is wrong with money? Our most straightforward answer should be, nothing. But it seems that when money gets in contact with our nature, especially when we are placed in certain situations, we think that we can use it to define our relationships, secure ourselves, gain power positions, and buy our way through life. At one point in his life, the wisest of kings who ever lived said, "money is the answer for everything." (Ecclesiastes 10:19). But at a certain point, he came to himself and saw that all was "vanity" and "a vexation of spirit." He wrote as a conclusion to his great essay "fear God and keep his commandments, for this is the whole duty of man." (Ecclesiastes 12:13, 14).

Yes, even the wisest king had to learn that "money is" not "everything." If we lead in private or public, secular or religious life, we need to learn how to relate to money. We need to understand the significance of accountability and responsibility, morality and fidelity, and all that will help us to stand on a high wall of dignity and integrity with regards to money. As is often said, those who peddle and receive money should know that they are not only selling things but they are selling their souls. So here is what I ask, let us remember to keep our souls from corruption.

LEADING WITH AUTHORITY

What will people not do to gain power? The process of this election cycle has reconfirmed a lot that I have learned over the years. But this cycle has made it more transparent to me. The dishing out of criticisms, character assassinations, bashing of one another in advertising, the labeling, the changing of positions, all make it seem that the people who are seeking power will do anything to gain it. The same observation can be made as one takes note of some incredible social policies that are presented. The same might be said as one listens to the dogmatic assertions with some pretending to be stronger than others. And the same might be said with the offer of promises to make America the strongest nation on earth, with the most massive military budget, hardware, and army, etc.

I cannot judge the hearts of any who are fighting to be in the position of President of the United States, but it seems from my vantage point, at least, that the lust for power has taken priority over the spirit of service. At one time the call to the presidency placed the emphasis on service, but today, it seems it is prestige, position, and power.

Quite a few decades ago, ethicist Reinhold Niebuhr, who taught at Union Theological Seminary in New York City, focused on power and self-interest, as central themes in his teaching and writings. If he were alive today, I do not know what he might say, but it seems to me his thesis stands that as human beings we have an insatiable lust for power - the will to power, pride of power, social power, and spiritual power. The struggle among nations, the renewing of the arms race, and the exploitation of nature, and even what is seen among religious leaders are speaking to us of our insatiable desire for power.

My brief reflection simply seeks to ask those who are seeking leadership at the highest sphere of our nation, or leaders in any sphere to think of what the priority interest is as we find power. Do we think of power with the lustful desires of serving ourselves, or do we attempt to follow the way of Jesus to serve others? In speaking to his disciples Jesus reminded them they were not to do as the Gentiles do, in "lording" it over others. They were to remember that they are "servants" first (Luke 22:24-27, Matt. 20:20-28, Mark 10:35-45). That is to say that prestige, honorific titles, privilege, position, and power should take the lesser place to the spirit of serving.

Yes, real power - true power is I seen in the sphere of service. Real power is not what we perceive from our human area, but it is that which we get from God. He said through his prophet Zechariah to Zerubbabel, "Not by might, nor by power, but by My Spirit, says the Lord." (Zechariah 4:6). Real power is God who indeed gives. He sets up kings and kingdoms or presidents and rulers. He puts us in positions to serve. In the lust to rule many have set up themselves, but we who understand our calling from must know that real power is serving.

May we as leaders seek the grace of God so that we can have the right power priorities as we lead.

SEXUAL DISCRETION IN LEADERSHIP

A few years ago the Louisiana State elections were completed and John Bel Edwards won the governorship over Senator David Vitter. Vitter was considered the favorite until his supposed sexual indiscretion was brought into the open and used as an advertisement for the campaign. Although the advertisements drew a "drumbeat of criticism" about heavy-handed campaign tactics, they seemed to have had the intended effect as Vitter's negatives spiked among voters, and he lost the election.

It was somewhat startling to me that those ads should have had the impact they did since sexual indiscretions among leaders seem to be the norm today. After the epoch-making trial of President Bill Clinton, the resignation of house speaker, Newt Gingrich, the downfall of governor Mark Sanford, and their rehabilitation, it seems that sexual indiscretion among leaders is an accepted norm. So the result of the Louisiana election was quite surprising if the sexual indiscretion was all that made the difference. Of course, I am not seeking to trivialize the judgment of Louisianans, but to take note that my heart had a little gratification to know that despite the deterioration of social values, there are areas of the United States of America that say that deteriorated values are unacceptable. There are still people in America who hold leaders to a high standard of morality and expect them to behave with integrity and dignity in sexual matters.

When leaders are not able to maintain integrity and dignity in sexual matters they often cause great hurt to themselves and those they lead. Think of King David, one of the most revered biblical kings, when he got involved with Bathsheba, how he caused strife in his family and tragedy in the kingdom. His story appears with the sordid twist of a novel when it reports that David got involved in sexual indiscretion with Bathsheba, and then murdered her husband, Uriah (2 Samuel 11). Think of Samson, the giant judged of Israel, how much he and the people of Israel lost through his sexual indiscretions. Because of his sexual transgressions, the Israelites suffered much at the hands of the Philistines. Samson himself suffered when his eyes were plucked out and he was put into the Philistine jail for many years. To end his life of misery Samson committed suicide by pulling down the temple of Dagan with more than three thousand Philistines (Judges 16). In the assessment of his life, it is clear that Samson could have brought greater military victories to Israel, but he was weakened because of his lack of sexual discretion.

Yes, sexual indiscretions have profound impact on leaders, but not only on those we define as public leaders but on one and all. Multiple individuals have failed because they have allowed their lives to be controlled by sexual indiscretions. So let me conclude by asking a few simple questions:

> Do we use sex to coerce others?

Do we sex to manipulate others?
Do we use derogatory sexual language?
Do we use sex to put down others?
How do we view sex in our office spaces?
Do we use sex to gain power?

SPEAKING THE TRUTH IN LEADERSHIP

As leaders of the world assembled at the United Nations on September 28, and gave their speeches, I had an interest in listening to what the leaders of Iran, Russia, and the United States had to say. Not much surprised me, but one line from President Barack Obama's address profoundly struck me. "You can try to control access to information, but you cannot turn a lie into truth," he said. It brought me back to my elementary school days and the Gem attributed to H. W. Dolcken that we often recited; "Speak the truth, and speak it ever, cost it what it will; He who hides the wrong he did, does the wrong thing still." It also reminded me of the lines of poetry that Dr. Martin Luther King Jr. popularized from America's most celebrated romantic poet, James Russell Lowell; "Truth forever on the scaffold, wrong forever on the throne, yet that scaffold sways the future, and, behind the dim unknown, standeth God behind the shadow, keeping watch over his own." Dr. King also said, "We shall overcome because Carlisle is right. 'No lie can live forever.' We shall overcome because William Cullen Bryant is right. 'Truth crushed to earth will rise again.'"

What is my interest in focusing on the question of leaders telling the truth? I focus on this question because, in political or diplomatic speeches, we confront many falsehoods. In fact, as one who preaches and teaches the gospel of Christ, I seek to challenge myself with making sure I tell the truth. And I would hope that my fellow ministers of all persuasions within the Christian faith would feel the same burden. To make my point practical within the Christian frame, let me offer two questions for reflection.

1. How does one make Sunday into the Biblical Sabbath?
2. How does one state in absolute terms that the Shroud of Turin is the cloak into which Jesus was buried?

As a leader, one of the thoughts that has guided me is one that says, "The history of truth has ever been the record of a struggle between right and wrong. The proclamation of the gospel has ever been carried forward in this world in the face of opposition, peril, loss, and suffering." I am also reminded of a verse that I learned in our childhood home at family worship, "Lying lips are an abomination to the Lord, but they who speak truly are his delight" (Proverbs 12:22). This is to say in the context of my biblical reflection, that leaders need to be careful. They are to seek to:

1. Know the truth - (John 8:32)
2. Speak the truth (in love) (Ephesians 4:15)
3. Teach the truth (2 Timothy 2:15)
4. Avoid suppressing the truth (Romans 1:18)
5. Understand that only truth will bring true freedom. (John 8:32 and 33)

The responsibility of truth-telling, whether as a political leader, a news reporter, a scientist, a teacher, a pastor, a father, a mother or whoever else, is fundamental. The most profound reality we must face is that we cannot be sustained if we perpetuate a culture of lies. "The father of lies," likes a lie, but we are not to give him the chance to destroy our world with lies. Let us endeavor to uphold truth, for truth makes for a different kind of leadership.

LEADING WITH DETERMINATION

Allow me to begin my reflection with a Scriptural quote that is most relevant for the point concerning persistence in leadership, namely: "But the one who endures to the end, he will be saved." (Matthew 24:13). The quote focuses on "the end" of the world, as Jesus spoke of it, but it is true about the end of all things in which we are engaged. One of the most significant ingredients for success in any endeavor is persistence. Those who are presenting themselves as candidates in the contemporary cycle of the election culture must understand this well, at least they should. They likely have found out that the road to success is strewn with many pitfalls and oppositional forces, and if they do not know how to navigate the pitfalls and deal with the forces of opposition, they are doomed from the start; they will be frustrated and drop out.

What is true for those who are seeking to be elected is true for all of us. However, let me direct my thought to those of us who are leaders in our homes, churches and local communities because in such places, there is a profound need for persistence in leadership. Current social challenges indicate that some of us have lost the spirit of perseverance to correct negative behaviors and challenge poor attitudes. So for anyone who might be thinking of what it takes to be persistent, let me offer seven suggestions predicated on the word "endurance" that Jesus used in the text quoted above.

1. **Toughness** - Martin Luther King Jr. often spoke of the need to have "a tough mind" and "a tender heart" for effectiveness.
2. **Resolve** - The strong mind gives one resolve. It helps one to make up one's might to say, "This one thing I do."
3. **Resilience** - The strong mind also helps a person to bounce back. It helps one to say, "I can't give in or give up now." Yes, resilience is profoundly important.
4. **Robustness** - The strong mind has to be healthy and whole, or it enters into violence. We are hearing of so many people who are mentally unhealthy these that it is frightening. Mentally sick leaders are dangerous.
5. **Tolerance** - The strong mind also teaches a person how to be tolerant. Not everything will work in one's favor, but one needs to learn to accept conditions that one might not like; even disagreeable people.
6. **Patience** - The strong mind can even lead one to be patient. There is no contradiction between having a tough mind and a tender heart. The one without the other can easily lead an individual into all kinds of trouble.
7. **Serenity** - The mind that gets agitated too easily will find it hard to be persistent. Remember the Syro-Phonecian woman who came to Jesus? She made a request, and Jesus answered and said, "It is not good to take the children's bread and throw it to the dogs." "But she said, 'Yes, Lord; but even the dogs feed on the crumbs which fall from their masters' table.'" (see Matthew 15:25-27). The result is that she got what she wanted. Her serenity gave her the victory.

How are you as a leader in your home, church or community? Are you truly persistent? Are you determined? Please remember that "Persistence pays."

LEADING IN A TIME OF CRISIS

The constant struggle to deal with terrorism and financial dislocations, it is evident that just about every organization in our land is facing a crisis. It seems clear that anyone who is seeking to lead in our contemporary world must know how to lead through crises. Do I need to say more about the mess that we are facing today? I think not, except to note that our heightened fears, anxiety, monitoring of individuals, manifested prejudices, xenophobia, and other negative attitudes are evidences of the many crisis facing us.

In the midst of the crisis, I see in the political sphere, the frustrating search for leadership with a clear vision, that is, leaders who can inspire. But I wonder whether many of us are seriously consulting with God, or are we just caught up in the hype of promises and policies as they are being presented in language suitable to us?

Once again, I am using this medium to give an invitation to all who are reading this reflection to seek for divine wisdom. Pray that God will help us to select the right persons to lead us through the crisis we are in. When Egypt was in the plight of a famine, God elevated Joseph to become governor. The circumstances through which Joseph got to the position were strange. His brothers sold him as a slave to Midianite traders who took him to Egypt and traded him to Potiphar. While serving in Potiphar's house he was falsely accused and put in jail, but God got Joseph out of jail and allowed Pharaoh to promote him to the position of Governor of Egypt. By re-organizing the agricultural system of Egypt, Joseph was able to save Egypt and the neighboring nations through one of the fiercest time of famine ever known in recorded history.

What was it that made a difference in the leadership of Joseph? He had in him the Spirit of God. He had faith. He was courageous. He put away all prejudices and feelings of resentment. He learned to trust those about him. Read his compelling story in Genesis 39-42. You might also care to read about Moses in Exodus 3-14, and Daniel in Daniel 1-6. In these cases, that I have sighted, and so many more that I could mention, the constant theme is that those who lead best in crisis have learned to trust in God.

Let us pray God that we will be imbued with such Spirit today and that God will give us such leaders who have such a Spirit that we will not be led astray.

LEADING WITH RESPONSIBILITY

While listening to President Obama as he gave his final State of the Union address to the Congress, I took careful note that he did not spend time blaming others for what he considered the shortcomings of his leadership. Sure enough, he could have spent time insulting those who had pledged themselves to make him "a one-term president." He could have taken note that when their efforts failed they continued a program of consistent opposition to his propositions, but he did not make that a topic of interest. He could have talked about the resentment he felt from those who wished to delegitimize him as a born American citizen, but he did not. He could have pushed back against those who sought to trivialize him being the first black president, but he took a different road. As he spoke of his regret for not being able to unite the nation, he compared himself to two former presidents he thought might have done a better job. Whether or not one might agree with this kind of assessment, one cannot gainsay that his expression of humility and regret was one of the greatest moments in his speech.

If many of us were placed in the President's position we, likely, would have spent time boasting of our accomplishments, and then blasting those around us for the things we could not accomplish. Yes, blasting others for our failures is the way that a lot of leaders are engaging today. Such is, of course, the greatest temptation of the human spirit. Blaming others often reflects one's hurt pride, or lack of humility, and lack of taking responsibility. Only the strong and courageous are ever willing to stand up and restrain themselves from the temptations to blame. Elliot D. Cohen writing in *Psychology Today* says, "One of the most destructive human pastimes is playing the blame game. It has been responsible for mass casualties of war, regrettable acts of road rage, and on a broad interpersonal level (social, familial and work-related), a considerable amount of human frustration and unhappiness. The blame game consists of blaming another person for an event or state of affairs thought to be undesirable, and persisting in it instead of proactively making changes that improve the situation."

In a political culture where much time is spent in blaming, especially as it is thought of as a way to win an election, my simple encouragement to each one who reads this reflection is to stay away from the blame game and take responsibility for our every action. If all of us learn to take greater responsibility for our efforts, we will be more careful, from the start, about what we are about to do. Then we will be able to express our satisfaction in the words of the great Apostle Paul, "I have fought the good fight, I have finished the race, I have kept the faith. Finally, there is laid up for me the crown of righteousness, which the Lord, the righteous Judge, will give to me on that Day, and not to me only but also to all who have loved His appearing." (2 Timothy 4:7, 8 NKJV).

Yes, it is a blessing to stay away from playing the blame game. Let us all take more responsibility for our every action.

LEADING FROM THE PAST

I hate to hear it, even though I have had to tolerate it, leaders, who lead from the past by tearing down whoever has gone before. I have found it to be a temptation not only of secular leaders but those who lead in spiritual communities as well. When I hear colleagues doing it, it disturbs me and always allows me to ask myself how often have I fallen into the trap of speaking ill of those who have gone ahead of me in my pastoral charge.

There seems to be a penchant in the human heart for blaming those who have gone before, suggesting that they have not accomplished much, or anything at all. All they have done is leave the organization in a mess. If it is sounding like a contemporary form of leadership, that is how the current principal leader of the United States speaks. He makes constant references to the lack of accomplishments or poor accomplishments of the former president Barak Obama and other presidents before him. He states without verity that it is since he became president that anything has been done, I have heard him say stuff like, what has occurred did not happen in the last 50, if not a hundred years. When I hear his comments I sometimes say, he is "leading from the past."

My observation does not say that one should not evaluate the past and seek to rectify that which needs to be corrected. But it suggests that too much focus on the past can be tragic for any leader, or anyone who desires to get to the future. Some focus on history and speak of "the good old days" as if the present does not matter.

Everything good that has ever been accomplished happened in "the good old days" they say.

But to such, I point to the man of wisdom who says in Ecclesiastes 7:10 "Do not say, "Why were the former days better than these?" For you do not inquire wisely concerning this (NKJV). Many who talk of "the good old days," only need to take a closer look to see that the good old days were not so good, at all. The good old days had some of the same problems that are consistent with the challenges of the present.

Now, challenging those who like to speak of the past does not say, the past does not have significant value. Credited to the great philosopher, essayist, poet, and novelist George Santayana "Those who cannot remember the past are condemned to repeat it." God often encouraged his people, as we find in the prophet Isaiah, to remember the past. "Remember the former things of old: for I am God, and there is none else; I am God, and there is none like me, declaring the end from the beginning, and from ancient times the things that are not yet done, saying, my counsel shall stand, and I will do all my pleasure." (Isaiah 46:9-10 KJV). In Ecclesiastes, he advises, "Remember now your Creator in the days of your youth, Before the [a]difficult days come, and the years draw near when you say, "I have no pleasure in them" (Ecclesiastes 12:1 NKJV).

When one knows and acknowledges one's past history and also how God has dealt with his people in the past, it can open one's eyes to the present and even the future. Or let us say the past should not be used to restrict us, but to construct a positive way forward.

LEADING IN THE PRESENT

When we were children and were being trained to appreciate the significance of the present, we would often recite Anna Sewell poem, as published in *Black Beauty*, which says:

> "If you in the morning
> Throw minutes away,
> You can't pick them up
> In the course of a day.
> You may hurry and scurry,
> And flurry and worry,
> You've lost them forever,
> Forever and aye."

I remember, also, as children, how we would whisper a sentence at the ears of our peers and when they would turn and ask us what we said, we would answer, "Sorry, it pass you." That is, we were trying to get our peers to focus on the loss of opportunities.

Of course, the loss of the present opportunities is not a matter of child's play. There is something profoundly significant about the current or what is called today. That is, "Making hay while the sun shines." It is learning to deal with the present day, listening in the present, acting in the present, living in the present, leading in the present. And not waiting for tomorrow to do what needs to be done today. Not that one needs to burn out oneself in a day. Nor should one despise the past, because history often has profound lessons to teach us today. And today has an impact on the future. But the value of the present day (today) cannot be overstated.

Investors and accountants speak of the significance of "present value," and "future value." They take note of how the present value is used to build future value. And they emphasize that those who do not appreciate the present will fail of being useful in the future.

The Bible speaks much about the present day (today). For example, we read in Ecclesiastes 9:10 (NIV) "Whatever your hand finds to do, do it with all your might, for in the realm of the dead, where you are going, there is neither working nor planning nor knowledge nor wisdom." In Proverbs 27:1 (NKJV) we read, "Do not boast about tomorrow, for you do not know what a day may bring forth." In other parts of Scripture, we note the substance of texts focusing on today or the present. Thus, "Today is the day of salvation." "Today is the of God's favor." "Today is the acceptable day of opportunity." "Today, if you will hear his voice do not harden your hearts."

In effect, there is an insistence on knowing the value of the present day. Thus what can be done today should not be left until tomorrow. Decisions that are to be made today should not be left until tomorrow. Choices that are to be made today should not be moved to tomorrow.

Do not put off for tomorrow what is to be or can be done today. "Procrastination is the thief of time." It's natural to talk about tomorrow and things you've planned to do, but no one knows if tomorrow will even come for us. The only day we really have is today.

LEADING TO THE FUTURE

My children used to tell me that they think that I am psychic. They felt so because whenever I saw them following specific directions, I would say to them what the logical outcomes were going to be. If they insisted on a path, invariably, what I told them came to pass. I am not psychic. I do not have any evidence of that. And I am no prophet or the son of a prophet and do not claim that, but I find that it is essential as a father and a leader in the public community, to be able to make precise predictions of the future. By studying history, we are often able to predict the future. In which case I am able to take preventative actions or preempt any destructive action that might have been on the way.

I think the capacity to predict is especially crucial during this time of terroristic warfare. Many government leaders are working overtime to stop the most tragic activities that are being planned by extremist. Of course, it is of interest how predictions are being made in the current political discourse. It is a challenge for many leaders that they have no notion of how to predict the future. They go about life and struggle on their way until they land somewhere. Some put their trust in Horoscopes, Tarot Cards, Palm Readers, and other agents that of another source that the divine, then they wonder why it is that those who follow them end in failure or do not trust them. It is said that what makes for successful leadership is the capacity to project and see outcomes, by putting together goals that are realizable.

So if you wish to be useful in making predictions, and you are not a prophet so that you can consult like the ancients, especially when they were going to war, here are six things I suggest as part of a strategy for learning how to be effective at predicting the future.

1. Be very keen at how you listen to what is being said or happening around you
2. Learn the facts - Do not ignore them. To ignore the facts is to be suicidal
3. Use your own experiences and that of others about you. Do not be foolish, what has been will be. You are not the first to walk down any of life's road; somebody has gone there before and has faced certain consequences
4. Learn to discern - Discernment is a rear gift. It is not always a part of ordinary logic. True discernment comes from God
5. Inquire of the Spirit of God - Pray for the Lord to guide you. You might not have known that can be explained by any logical construction, but God has promised that the Spirit will guide you into all truths.
6. Use (sanctified) imagination - We can predict the future by imagining what the future will be and work to make it a possibility.
7. Be humble about what you see, because many contingencies can change the future. Even some of what the prophets said did not come about as was predicted. Circumstances change. People repent. God has a different plan.

Yes, in the ultimate, the future belongs only to God. However, he has given us clues and the capacity to enter into the future. If we want to be successful, let's not be afraid of peering into the future as a part of our strategy in leadership.

LEADING WITH CONFIDENCE

During the present presidential campaign, across our land, we are being bombarded by miscellany promises from the varied individuals presenting themselves to be elected. And because people are saying they are profoundly disappointed and angry because of the broken promises from current politicians; candidate politicians, or some who are trying to avoid the label of a politician, are coming along and making more "fantastic" promises. Most are saying they are trying to distinguish themselves from the political system; they are much more to be trusted than the "scoundrels" who have gone before and who have not fulfilled their promises. But, it seems to me, that the more fantastic and utopian the promises of the present candidates, the more some people seem to be drawn to them. I wish I could be more helpful to the many who are on the edge of future frustrations by reminding them of the Scriptural notes:

> It is better to take refuge in the LORD than to trust in humans. - Psalm 118:8

> It is better to take refuge in the LORD than to trust in princes. - Psalm 118:9

> Thus says the Lord: "Cursed *is* the man who trusts in man and makes flesh his strength, whose heart departs from the Lord - Jeremiah 17:5

From what I have said, you might be thinking that I am against leaders who make promises. Let me answer that while I offer much caution to leaders on the kinds of promises they make, and to people on the promises they believe, I am not against promises. I do think that leaders should make promises. But let me also offer the following 16 suggestions to every leader and any leader, whether politician or pastor, parent or public administrator.

1. Promise to tell the truth
2. Promise to be faithful
3. Promise to be clear about expectations
4. Promise to be consistent
5. Promise to be ethical
6. Promise to be honest
7. Promise to be transparent
8. Promise to be graceful
9. Promise to speak well of others
10. Promise to have a positive attitude
11. Promise to create structures that build confidence and respect
12. Promise to own up to responsibilities
13. Promise to learn what matters in life
14. Promise to be authentic and vulnerable
15. Promise to be more realistic
16. Promise to admit limitations

I offer the above because I know that leadership is hard, and because I am cognizant of the fact that a leader is always called to provide expectations and make grand promises. But I find the need still to caution myself not to provide more than I can fulfill. As one who has been in leadership for nearly a half a century, I also find the need to make it clear that while there are daily pressures to change my promises, I have to be persistent in making sure that what I promise is carried to a finish.

Promises! Promises!! Promises!!! God makes many of them, and he fulfills them. We should all remember that our complete trust is to be in God, not in human beings.

PUTTING PEOPLE DOWN

I watched the Democratic Debate this week because I wanted to take note of the kind of leadership that each candidate would provide for the country. I also watched one of the Republican Debates. My most significant take away from the debate this week was not in all of the policy presentations, for which I noted some of the candidates were so well prepared, but what struck me much was the robust response from Senator Bernie Sanders to the persistent discussions about Secretary Hillary Clinton's emails. He insisted that he did not wish to spend all of his time on the emails, and challenged the media and those who are wasting so much time trying to tear others down, to stop the charade. I am not reciting here, the direct phrase that Senator Sanders used, but I find it frustrating that ongoing discussions in the media and among some of the presidential candidates are focused on the putting down of one another.

This reflection takes note of the fact that as leaders, we can hold the truth high without putting people down. Jesus did just that. He challenged those in his time, who sought, through racial prejudices or whatever else they used, to put others down. He challenged them to deal lovingly with those they considered "dogs." He challenged them about their attitudes toward aliens, the less fortunate, the defenseless, the disinherited, the downtrodden and those who were perceived as ignorant. Think of how Jesus treated children and their mothers who came to see him? Think of how he treated women? Think of how he treated Gentiles like the Syro-Phonecian woman and the Centurion? Yes, He not only challenge those in the structures of leadership, but also the disciples he was training to become leaders of his church. There are many Scriptural texts to underline the above points, but the one text I want us to note carefully is, "Do unto others as you would have them do to you" (Luke 6:31).

As church or public community leaders, if we are ever tempted to put others down we need to ask ourselves:

1. How do we feel when people try to put us down?
2. How many honorable friends are we making by putting others down?
3. How much are we winning by putting others down?
4. How do we feel when we make mistakes, and others try to put us down?
5. How do we feel when we are good at something, and people put us down?
6. How much are we contributing to the culture of disrespect, hate, and violence when we put other people down?
7. What kind of influence are we sharing with the next generation when we practice putting others down?

The challenging point is that putting other people down does not help to build us up or build up our society. So let us spend more time to build other people up. Put others first, and we will be with them in first place. In the final analysis, remember that God will judge those who seek to put others down.

BUILDING OTHER PEOPLE UP

The struggle to face the brokenness and destruction of our community has been a profound concern since the latter half of the last century. In fact, in all of the free world, many social scientists are asking, "How can balance our rights and responsibilities, our privacy and the public good.? How can we balance law and order? How can we balance the opportunity to protest with respect? How can we balance tolerance with trust? "

Some individuals have given their responses by suggesting that we need to learn to live with chaos instead of community. Those projecting this view seem to resign themselves to the thinking that there is nothing that can be done to retake us from chaos into community.

In some sense, I do agree that in the world, as it is, we will have to learn how to live with chaos. However, it is also my conviction that God has given to us the greatest of responsibility, to do all we can to help rebuild the great gift of community. It is also my conviction that as leaders in our homes, churches and public life, that we need to show by our attitude and behavior, that community is a possibility. I do not know that any of you who read this reflection will care for a Bible study, but here are a few Scriptural texts for contemplation. Please take note that the textual quotations were recited by Jesus Christ, Himself to the disciples or written by the Apostles as they sought harmony in the Early Christian Community. The texts are still beneficial to us if we are willing to use them.

- *Mark 9:50 - "Salt is good; but if the salt becomes unsalty, with what will you make it salty again? Have salt in yourselves, and be at peace with one another."*
- *John 13:14 - "If I then, the Lord and the Teacher, washed your feet, you also ought to wash one another's feet.*
- *John 13:34 - "A new commandment I give to you, that you love one another, even as I have loved you, that you also love one another.*
- *John 13:35 - "By this, all men will know that you are My disciples if you have love for one another."*
- *John 15:12 - "This is My commandment, that you love one another, just as I have loved you.*
- *Romans 12:10 - Be devoted to one another in brotherly love; give preference to one another in honor;*
- *Romans 12:16 - Be of the same mind toward one another; do not be haughty in mind, but associate with the lowly. Do not be wise in your own estimation.*
- *Romans 13:8 - Owe nothing to anyone except to love one another; for he who loves his neighbor has fulfilled the law.*
- *Romans 14:13 - Therefore let us not judge one another anymore, but rather determine this--not to put an obstacle or a stumbling block in a brother's way.*
- *Romans 14:19 - So then we pursue the things which make for peace and the building up of one another.*

- *Romans 15:5 - Now may the God who gives perseverance and encouragement grant you to be of the same mind with one another according to Christ Jesus,*
- *Romans 15:7 - Therefore, accept one another, just as Christ also accepted us to the glory of God.*

Let us not forget that if we cannot help to build community, we will be working for our destruction.

LEADING WITH INTEGRITY

Integrity, which means that a character is "intact," is an invaluable possession. According to an article that I read some time ago, "When something is well built, we say it has integrity." If in an earthquake a building survives without cracking or shifting, we say it has structural integrity. When something physically collapses, we mean it didn't have the integrity to withstand the impact. That is to say; one never knows when something or someone reflects a character of integrity until it passes through a crisis. One never knows whether something or someone has integrity if all is normal. In effect, excessive pressure tells much about one's integrity of character.

My present reflection is not so much on the integrity of things but is primarily connected to my ongoing interest in speaking of leadership that makes a difference. It is of importance, to me, that so few leaders within our contemporary culture seem to have the kind of character that one can say that is a person of integrity. How can such persons make a significant impact on the world if they have no integrity? How can they bring about positive change? What effect are they bringing to the youth of this generation if they have no integrity? How can they build trust in the culture if they are creating such lack of confidence? If one is to follow the polls and listen to the ongoing discussions concerning the leaders of our times, one might be convinced that there are very few leaders with integrity, especially within the political sphere.

Yes, the transformation of our present society demands leaders with integrity. It needs leaders:

1. With stellar characters
2. Who will not sell out
3. Who are faithful to high (or holy) values in their consciences
4. Who are genuinely moral in all relationships
5. Who are willing to take responsibility for every action?
6. Who are accountable to those about them?
7. Who are willing to stand up for truth and principles regardless of the poles
8. Who are not prepared, like Congressman Paul Ryan, said, to trade family for fame
9. Who are not just interested in power and positions but principles
10. Who are faithful to God and their divine calling?

These qualities of character are not only important for public leaders, of course, but are needful for all of us. Too many of us are failing to understand that the crisis of leadership being faced in our public society, our churches, and our homes, is the result from the distrust of the integrity of leadership, which is consistent with our times. We must understand this that we cannot make the societal or relational progress we ought to until we have integrity. Indeed, integrity is something that money cannot buy.

VALUING SPIRITUALITY IN LEADERSHIP

Spirituality in leadership, "Does it make for a different kind of leadership?" This is a question being brought to the fore in the present presidential election cycle. One candidate held up his Bible for a couple of weeks proclaiming that it was the most significant book in his life. After specific questions were raised concerning what he knew about the Bible, he seemed to have felt a bit ashamed that he was not able to give a vigorous defense of himself and since then, has stopped waving the Bible. However, he began to question another candidate's religion, which has elevated the discussion on spirituality.

My interest, of course, is not to discuss the faith or spirituality of any particular candidate in the election cycle, but to ask whether religion or spirituality does make a difference in the way that one is expected to lead? If one were to ask some contemporary Evangelicals the question, the answer might be an immediate, "Yes." But the problem is not just for Evangelicals, but also for all of us. Does spirituality make a difference in leadership?

In fact, when I speak of spirituality, I am not just talking of people's religious persuasion, regarding religion or denomination or sect affiliation, but of the depth of relationship that one has with God. Some individuals say, "I am spiritual, I am not religious." This is an interesting distinction and one which those who understand what religion is will not necessarily agree. However, that might be, those who write dictionaries will say that **spirituality** is a broad concept with room for many perspectives. However, they seem to agree that it includes a sense of connection to something bigger than ourselves, and it typically involves a search for meaning in life. As such, it is a universal human experience—something that touches us all. For those who take the description with utter seriousness, I would say that it has a profound impact on their respect for God, on their prayer life, their faith life, their morality, their responsibility and their relationship with others.

If the latter is true, then we can conclude that spirituality makes a profound difference in leadership. And that is not just for leadership in a spiritual community as the church but in public leadership. Thus when Joseph was brought to Pharaoh to interpret his dream concerning a coming famine, Pharaoh sensed the seriousness of the interpretation, and immediately knew that he needed a wise hand to help him prepare for the disaster. He consulted with his wise men and asked, "Can we find anyone like this man, one in whom is the spirit of God" (Genesis 41:38)? The wise men responded in the affirmative concerning Joseph, and so Pharaoh said to Joseph, "Since God has informed you of all this, there is no one so discerning and wise as you are" (Cf. Genesis 41:39). The same is true about Daniel. After the mysterious handwriting on the wall and Belshazzar was searching for an interpreter, the queen mother came to Belshazzar and said, "There is a man in your kingdom who has the spirit of the holy gods in him. In the time of your father, he was found to have insight and intelligence and wisdom like that of the gods. Your father, King Nebuchadnezzar, appointed him chief of the magicians, enchanters, astrologers, and diviners" (Daniel 5:11).

Yes, if one is genuinely spiritual, such a person can be expected to speak the truth about issues, instead of engaging in political parsing. He/she should challenge the structures of evil, instead of upholding them, and bless others, instead of cursing them. Yes, spirituality does make for a different kind of leadership.

SHOWING STRENGTH IN LEADERSHIP

I was listening to my favorite secular radio station, CSpan, and heard the replay of quite a few of the presidential candidates' speeches at the Iowa State Fair, with each projecting themselves as strong. Some talked about how they would fix the economy; others about building a wall at the border between Mexico and the US, and others spoke about what they would do to demonstrate that the USA could overcome Isis and all of the enemies of the United States in the Middle East and across the world. Some thought that the more they raised the tone of their voices, the more they could persuade prospective voters that they were strong.

The point that was most evident from the speeches and the media analysis is that people are looking for strong leadership. Most of the presidential candidates, who spoke, particularly from the Republican side, were quite nostalgic in invoking the name of President Ronald Regan as a strong leader. They indicated that they desired to model him, versus Presidents Carter or Obama. After listening to them, I began to ask myself "What is strength in leadership?" On deeper reflection, I concluded that it had more to do with character rather than the projection of personality or brute force. I do not know what you think of the character of the Presidents Reagan, Carter or Obama. I am not giving my evaluation here, and do not wish to join those who are testing their political ideologies and competing personalities. I do have just one agreement with them, namely that the world is in need of influential leaders, that is, people who can make a difference.

Moses, the great leader of Israel, who is used quite often as a model of leadership, also believed that strength was needed to lead. He brought a challenge to Joshua when he said, "Be strong and of a good courage, fear not, nor be afraid of them: for the Lord thy God, he it is that doth go with thee; he will not fail thee, nor forsake thee." (Deuteronomy 31:6 King James Version). Joshua thought of the importance of what was said that he recorded it in the first chapter of his book. "Have not I commanded thee? Be strong and of a good courage; be not afraid, neither be thou dismayed: for the Lord thy God is with thee whithersoever thou goest." (Joshua 1:9 King James Version).

Whatever else Moses might have meant, it is clear to me, that his understanding of strength was not so much what the popular culture was projecting, but rather that of character and the connection of people with their God. Yes, resistance is not brute force; it is not so much physical ability or the ability to give persuasive speeches or offer fictional promises, as is being projected in the prevailing culture; strength is found in one's character and one's spiritual connection with God.

We might note this from Scripture that while the Apostle Paul was not the most imposing character and evidently did not have the greatest of physical strength; he had a brave character that drove the passion of the Christian mission. From that perspective, he reminded the Corinthians of what God said to him, "My grace is sufficient for you, for my power is made perfect in weakness." "Therefore," he says, "I will boast all the more gladly about my weaknesses, so that Christ's power may rest on me." (2 Corinthians 12:9). This is a powerful conclusion, and we will do well to focus on it. All of us who are leaders in our homes, or our religious and public communities, have given so much wrong definition to strength that we allow for too much violence in the world. In effect, we are strong not because we talk tough, or become reckless in our actions, but because we understand our connection to the divine who is willing to work for us in the in how we need to make a difference.

THE COMPASSION FACTOR IN LEADERSHIP

The capacity to love, respect, and relate intensely to other people is referenced as compassion. I take note of this because I have been wondering what is happening to such capacity from what we are seeing in our contemporary culture, especially as we see and hear the expressions and reactions to some of our public leaders. Is the spirit of compassion being eroded from our culture? How are we reacting to people who think differently from us? What concerns do we have for the hundreds or thousands of children separated from their immigrant parents? How are we relating to our neighbors? How are we responding to those who are being profiled as our enemies? How are we treating orphans, widows and the oppressed in our midst? Are we concerned for them? Are we stopping seriously to think about them? Are we feeling any pain about their condition?

It is time that every one of us, who have influence or are spreading any influence, to ask ourselves the above questions. It seems clear that we are in a time when our culture is developing strains of resentment and hatred that hark back to times in our history about which we cannot be proud. The number of public movements that are emerging to combat the erosion of compassion is somewhat gratifying, but it is not enough to look to the general movements to transform our hearts. Each of us must look into our own heart and ask ourselves whether or not we have the kind of attitude and motivation for reaching out to others or are our lives just all about us.

Yes, to be compassionate we need to check our heart regularly and find the pockets where ego drives us to do uncompassionate things. We cannot only be concerned about ourselves but must also show concern for others. When we pray, it needs to be more than a prayer about our interests. I heard about one father praying, "Lord bless me, my wife, Mary and George, us four and no more." All he wanted was a blessing on his family. This might seem trite, but some people pray like that. But to be genuinely compassionate we need to reach beyond our families, beyond our kin, and even beyond our friends, who are well known to us. Each of us needs to test our prejudices and seek to transform them.

This is why Jesus said:

> "You have heard that it was said, 'You shall love your neighbor and hate your enemy.' But I say to you, love your enemies, bless those who curse you, do good to those who hate you, and pray for those who spitefully use you and persecute you, that you may be sons of your Father in heaven; for He makes His sun rise on the evil and on the good, and sends rain on the just and on the unjust. For if you love those who love you, what reward have you? Do not even the tax collectors do the same? Matthew 5:43-46 NKJV)

Indeed, compassion is a compelling character trait to have in one's life and our social systems. It has been shown that leaders who have compassion are more effective and transformative than those who lack empathy. Jesus, as we have seen from his teachings, was the master of compassion. If we will follow his way of compassion, we will transform our lives and our culture.

THE FAITH FACTOR IN LEADERSHIP

I was interacting with a group of leaders some time ago. In listening to their different perspectives with regards to the progress that was possible in their organization, I was amazed to hear the similarities. Most were emphasizing all of the obstacles or blockers that they were facing, thus allowing them to make the kinds of decisions they were doing. Their desires were not being accomplished; they felt frustrated that they had to be accommodating rather poor alternatives.

As I thought of the obstacles they were naming, I began to reflect on Moses with Israel at the Sea of Reed (The Red Sea). Israel was trapped between two plateaus, namely Migdol, a watchtower on their left and the other, Baal Zephon, a temple mount with towers on their right. Before them was the sea, and behind was the pursuing Egyptian army of Pharaoh with 600 chariots, horses with their riders and thousands of foot soldiers. As Israel looked at the situation, their hearts sank, and they cried out to the Lord but voiced their desire to Moses that they would have preferred to have died in Egypt rather than being led to their death in the wilderness. At that point, Moses cried to the Lord who offered the greatest encouragement of Moses' life. I love to read it and also to preach it as it is recorded in Exodus 14:13-18:

> 13 And Moses said to the people, "Do not be afraid. Stand still, and see the salvation of the Lord, which He will accomplish for you today. For the Egyptians whom you see

today, you shall see again no more forever. **14** The Lord will fight for you, and you shall hold your peace." **15** And the Lord said to Moses, "Why do you cry to Me? Tell the children of Israel to go forward. **16** But lift up your rod, and stretch out your hand over the sea and divide it. And the children of Israel shall go on dry *ground* through the midst of the sea. **17** And I indeed will harden the hearts of the Egyptians, and they shall follow them. So I will gain honor over Pharaoh and over all his army, his chariots, and his horsemen. **18** Then the Egyptians shall know that I *am* the Lord, when I have gained honor for Myself over Pharaoh, his chariots, and his horsemen." (NKJV).

Moses did as God told him and the Israelites passed through the Red Sea on dry land, while the Egyptians drowned in the flooding waters.

What is it about Moses that allowed him to make such a difference as a leader? He was able to see a way out of no way. It was not with his human eye, but he put his faith in God, thus making the impossible into the possible. The word "faith" which I have used is a naughty word these days in our unbelieving, secularist and egotistical culture. To have faith is to seem weak. But that is precisely what Moses did. He had faith and lifted his rod to God, and the sea divided into two walls. The Israelites were able to pass through on dry land. This was only one of the many incidents in which Moses was involved as he led the people to the borders of Canaan. By faith, he was also able to see water flowing from a rock. He also saw manna and quails for the people.

Yes, the power of faith, not just any faith, as we hear it in the universal lingua franca, but faith in God. It made Moses one of the most effective leaders this world has ever seen, and it does, and can make a profound difference.

THE GRACE FACTOR IN LEADERSHIP

There is a cream advertised for women called The Grace Factor. It is touted to be one of the most effective creams to make women look younger and superfluously beautiful. I have seen the advertisement, and do not wish to contend with the advertisers since I am not in cream testing and know that many other creams are advertised the same. No, I am not seeking to pit one cream against others. I leave the contention and comparison to the advertisers. But the concept of "the grace factor" is profoundly attractive to me.

My interest in "the grace factor" focuses on something more than a cream. My thoughts are directed to the power of the most marvelous and transformative gift that has been given to humanity to cover our sins. God also gives us grace to bring about healing in all our relationships, to open the way of forgiveness, to help us in the midst of our suffering, to transform our service and direct our lives toward positive outcomes.

Because of some of the graceless attitudes that are being displayed in the actions of many of our contemporary leaders, I am pressed to invite you to think of the difference it makes when grace impacts leadership. The Apostle Paul who has been called "the apostle of grace" says, grace makes a difference in all of life. He uses the grace concept 114 times throughout his Epistles. For example, in his Epistles are included "grace and peace" (Romans 1:7; 1 Corinthians 1:3; 2 Corinthians 1:2; Ephesians 1:2; Philippians 1:2; Colossians 1:2;

1 Thessalonians 1:1; 2 Thessalonians 1:2), as his primary greeting. In his farewells, he speaks of, "The grace of our Lord Jesus Christ (Philippians 4:23; 2 Corinthians 13:14). He takes note throughout his Epistles that a person is justified by faith through grace (Romans 3:24). He notes that one who lives in freedom does so under the "dispensation of grace" (Ephesians 20:24). One who lives does so "under grace instead of under law" (Romans 6:14). Then, he makes clear that salvation is not something about which we need boast because it is by grace. "For by grace you have been saved through faith, and that not of yourselves; *it is* the gift of God, not of works, lest anyone should boast" (Ephesians 2:8, 9 **NKJV**).

In effect, on the final point, it is easy to boast when as persons or leaders we feel successful at what we have set forth to accomplish. But we called to remember that when any pride raises that what is achieved is not so much what we have done as much as it is what God has done through us. In the context of leadership, we say a graceful leader knows how to share the credit. A graceful leader acknowledges how much of his/her accomplishments are built on the work of others or in cooperation with others. These are facts we too often forget and take credit where we should not.

The point is that graceful leaders know how to be grateful to God and those who bless them. Graceful leaders know how to admit their weaknesses and pardon the failings of others. Graceful leaders recognize their fallibility and that those about them need their gracious support. Yes, grace makes the most significant difference in the lives of successful human being, and the context of our reflection, on leaders and effective organization.

TAKING ADVISE WHEN YOU LEAD

This morning for my devotional, I read 1 Kings 12, a story with which I am quite familiar. But on rereading it, it came to me with a new impress as I have been thinking of the ongoing presidential campaign. The story is that of Rehoboam, King Solomon's son, who was to be installed on the throne following his father's death. At the assembly for the coronation, the people's emissaries requested specific reforms in the tax policy followed by Solomon. In order to facilitate his extravagant lifestyle, and build palaces for his many wives and concubines, Solomon had put a hefty tax burden on the people. The tax reforms requested by the people was to reduce the royal treasury and its power to continue the magnificence of Solomon's court. When Rehoboam listened to the request for reform, he asked for a few days so that he could seek counsel. He then went to the men who had counseled with his father. We are not sure whether the elders told Rehoboam to accept the people's demands, but they advised him to speak to the people civilly. But Rehoboam must have been uncomfortable with the counsel of the older men and therefore sought counsel from his peers who advised him to show no weakness to the people and to tax them even more then his father had done. He then went to the people with a proclamation thus:

> "Whereas my father laid upon you a heavy yoke, so shall I add tenfold to it. Whereas my father chastised (tortured) you with whips, so shall I chastise you with scorpions, for my littlest

finger is thicker than my father's loins; and your backs, which bent like reeds at my father's touch, shall break like straws at my own touch."

The rest of the story is that the people of Israel rebelled. The two tribes, Judah and Benjamin, remained with Rehoboam; and ten tribes went to Jeroboam about whom it was predicted that one day he would be king.

One of the central points of the story is that although the kingdom was already breaking up, yet accepting wise counsel could have kept it together much longer under Rehoboam's rule.

Yes, in leading in any sphere - home, church or the public square - it is critical to listen to wise counsel. Not every word of counsel works, but the wise person will seek to gain wisdom from others and find the will of the divine.

Here are a few significant scriptural quotes that should be ever kept in mind:

> He did evil in the sight of the LORD like the house of Ahab, for they were his counselors after the death of his father, to his destruction. - 2 Chronicles 22:4.

> Where there is no guidance the people fall, but in abundance of counselors there is victory - Proverbs 11:14.

> For by wise guidance you will wage war, and in abundance of counselors, there is victory - Proverbs 24:6.

What kind of counsel are you listening to? Do you listen to wise counsel? Or foolish counsel? Do you listen to any counsel at all?

TAKING THE FIRE WHEN YOU LEAD

In the ongoing, elongated presidential race, it is clear that some of the candidates have already become very, very, weary. Some seem true to their hearts and dropped out. Others seem to be able to accept the ridicule and scorn and are staying in. Some who are waiting seem determined to win. I have heard it said in a lottery advertisement, "You have to be in it to win it." To this, I say, "true." Of course, just being in it does not necessarily mean that one will win. In the processes of election and leadership, one needs to keep the "fire in the bones."

The loss of fire in the bones is not so unusual, and not unique to presidential candidates. Leaders all over will tell you that such is the challenge for us all. Church members will say the same, that there are times when they have lost the excitement and the fun. There is no fire in their bones. Even prophets of the Lord can lose the fire in the bones. Remember the prophet, Jeremiah? He was doing all he could to warn the people of God of the coming disaster because of their rebellion. Instead of listening to him, they mocked him. He became so discouraged that he decided to shut up his mouth and not repeat a word. But soon he looked within himself and said, "If I say, I will not mention him, or speak any more in his name, there is in my heart, as it were, a **burning fire shut up in my bones**, and I am weary with holding it in, and I cannot" (Jeremiah 20:9 ESV).

Yes, the questions that I wish to ask you as a reader is, do you have any fire in your bones? Do you have God in your heart? Is what you are doing inspired by God? Do you understand that God is the real fire in the bones? If what you are doing is God inspired, did you realize that it gives a different kind of energy to accomplish it? Here are the questions framed in more personal ways. Ask them to yourself as you go through this day.

1. Who or what is motivating me to do what I am doing? Is it God or friends?
2. Why am I doing what I am doing? Am I doing it in services to God or for myself?
3. Am I genuinely concerned with those about me why I am doing what I am doing?
4. Whose values am I uplifting why I am doing what you I am doing?

Yes, leadership needs "fire in the heart," or "fire in the bones." One might have talent, but one might lack fire, that is passion or power. But fire creates excellent dynamism. The fire brings joy, warmth, energy, courage, and leads us to overcome fear.

Yes, fire in the heart leads away from laziness. It truly makes for a different kind of leader.

THE CHARISMA OF LEADERSHIP

The Pope is being referenced in America, and across the world as the most charismatic personality there is. There is a lot of excitement, wherever he travels. News analysts constantly put forth a sole question on him as to "what makes him a different leader"? I am fascinated by the question since it is very connected to the one that one I like to pursue myself, namely, "What makes for a difference in leadership?" In watching the Pope, I have observed four things that are pertinent to what makes for a difference for effective leaders. You do not need to question whether I venerate the Pope. I am a Protestant in the radical sense of the term, but here are a few points that the slightest of enthusiasts can see, namely that:

1. **This Pope knows people**. He knows what makes people "tick." He feels them. He identifies with people without much effort. He is not one for the palace but the people. He understands diversity. He knows who his flock is and those who can be inspired by his words.
2. **This Pope knows his agenda**. He understands that in going across the world, and in coming to the United States, he is going to meet people with a variety of plans. He went to Cuba and met with Fidel Castro. He went to the White House and met with the President. He spoke to a joint session of Congress and spoke to Democrats and Republicans. He will see and hear from people of different religious persuasions. As

can be noted, many have sought and will seek to get him to focus on their agendas, but it is clear that he will not be persuaded; he knows what he is about.

3. **This Pope knows that he has a short time to do what he needs to do.** He is 78 years old. When he was elected a little over a year ago at age 77 he indicated that he might retire "early" and be off to the Father's house. Whatever else that early might mean, is likely of interest to some persons. What should be clear to all is that even popes die. And it is good that every one of us, no matter how respected we are, recognize our frailty.

4. **This Pope knows that he wants to leave a legacy.** Undoubtedly, it is for the revival and reformation of the Catholic Church. There is no question that what he is saying and doing will have a profound impact on the Church for generations. He is the 266th Pope, and it seems clear that he does not want to be remembered as a maintenance leader but as a transformational leader.

Yes, the Pope is clear. He is precise about what he wants to accomplish. He is very directed. He is a Pope of many firsts. He is the first Jesuit Pope. He is the first Latin American Pope. He is the first to call for mercy and compassion for Catholics who have been divorced, had abortions and have different sexual orientations. He is the first Pope to address a joint session of the United States Congress. He is the first to perform a canonization on American soil. He does not live in the usual residence of the popes, but in the simple place in which he stayed when he was elected.

The Pope engages effectively with Millennials by his excellent use of Twitter. Because of his concern for the less fortunate, he invited Catholic priests in Argentina to go into the slums and serve the people, thus he is known as the "Slum Pope." He does not dress in the flashy styles of other popes, but a modest dress; this gives a clear distinction of his different style. He carries a pastoral and a political message wherever he goes. He deeply respects the United States of America and is working hard for its heightened connection with the Holy Sea.

One word that is used among many to describe this Pope is "unique." Yes, he is a charismatic pope. He is considered the most influential man in the world. Whatever you think of the pope, you have to admit that he is a most effective leader.

THE DIGNITY OF LEADERSHIP

In my reflection on the ongoing political discourse each week, I am drawn again to comment on the tragic direction in which we are heading in the kind of leadership that we might have for the future. Even if those who are now so engaged in what is being called "Gutter Politics," the impact of their words and activities are bound to create a long-lasting effect on our culture that will take generations to repair.

The gutter, as we know, is the channel that is at the side of the road or the edge of a roof leading away what is considered the wastewater or garbage. When we say a person is in the gutter it means that the person is living life in a horrible way. When we speak of "Gutter Press," we say that the press has passed beyond the boundary of dignity and integrity, thus printing stories dominated by offensive sex and crime. One who is in the gutter has lost respect. Such a person engages in vileness and anything that is crude and rude.

Therefore, whether we speak of "gutter politics," "gutter press" or "gutter what-have-you," I am simply challenging us about the state of our society and the alternatives for leadership that are being presented to us today. I am happy to join those who are calling for a higher standard of discourse for it has been a great concern for me when one leader seeks to outdo another in the use of "Gutter Language." When that is the case, what might we think is happening to our social system? Is it clear to those who are so engaging that they are opening Pandora's box? That is, spreading feathers that they will not find it easy to collect. Are enough of us willing to say that one does not need to roll with another in the gutter to prove how tough one is? Is it being understood that this engagement in the gutter is not a game that we need to play like the game, "Roll in the mud, like a pig?" Do prospective leaders realize how lasting an effect "Gutter behavior" will have on our society and succeeding generations?

As a leader who believes in the dignity of humanity, I am asking whether we are building leadership in our society that will facilitate our true identity or will drag us into the wastes? May God help us to think clearly and forcefully of the way that we are seeking to go. The author of the biblical book of Ephesians gives this word of instruction that I believe can be a helpful guide not only to those of us who are religious leaders but even to public leaders. It reads:

"Let no corrupting talk come out of your mouths, but only such as is good for building up, as fits the occasion, that it may give grace to those who hear. And do not grieve the Holy Spirit of God, by whom you were sealed for the day of redemption. Let all bitterness and wrath and anger and clamor and slander be put away from you, along with all malice. Be kind to one another, tenderhearted, forgiving one another, as God in Christ forgave you" (Ephesians 4:29-32 ESV).

Yes, as we seek to lead, let us stay out of the gutter or make us think of the appropriateness of George Bernard Shaw's words, "I learned long ago, never to wrestle with a pig. You get dirty, and besides, the pig likes it." Live with dignity, never get in the mud.

THE CORRUPTING INFLUENCE OF LEADERSHIP

I do not want to blame every leader for the corruption that is evident in many, although it has been said, "Power corrupts and absolute power corrupts absolutely." Many leaders who are corrupted have had the seeds of corruption planted in them before they became leaders. Their narcissism, their prevarication, their lack of integrity, their immorality, and the lack of a sense of equity, have been in them all along. But leadership has a way of accelerating and exacerbating what grows from the seeds within. Or put another way, leadership has a corrupting potency which is sometimes not sensed when people are in other contexts of life.

One example to which I point in this direction is Saul, the king of Israel. Remember him? He was the tallest man in Israel. But when the people were searching for him to anoint him king, he hid in the haystacks in his father's barn. He was shy, very anxious and reluctant, but they found him and made him king. At the start of his reign, Saul was humble and opened to listening to the divine directive through the prophet Samuel. In fact, at one point the spirit of God came upon him and he prophesied, to the extent people began to ask, "Is Saul also among the prophets?"

However, after Saul began his reign as king, his real character came out. He won a few battles and started to become so arrogant that he often rejected divine counsel. In a battle with the Philistines, Saul's fearful spirit came out loud that he could not confront the Philistine giant, Goliath. However, at the moment of humiliation, a little shepherd "boy," named David, came on the scene, to visit his brothers. He was told of Israel's plight, and he offered to enter into the battle. When he was taken to Saul, Saul allowed him to fight the Philistine giant Goliath. And what seemed like Israel's defeat turned into a glorious victory with David killing the giant Goliath. The women began to sing, "Saul has slain his thousands and David his ten thousand." This action by the women led to the stimulation of Saul's impulsive spirit and resentment of David. Saul's resentment grew and grew until he did all he could to kill David. He became so corrupted and idolatrous that the spirit of God left him. The end of his life's story is that after the death of the prophet Samuel, Saul consulted with "the Witch of Endor" who predicted his death. In facing the loss of his final battle on Mount Gilboa against the Philistines, Saul requested his servant to kill him. When the servant did not kill him, Saul fell upon his sword and died. Read his story in 1st Samuel.

This story of King Saul is rather pathetic, but sadly, it has been repeated many times in history. Some leaders hate to deal with people with characters more upright than theirs. They will do all they can to stain other people's characters or seek to caricature them, call them names, or project upon them, to get others around them to despise that the ones they resent. Other leaders might even hate those around them who are as gifted, or more gifted as than they are, as wealthy as they are, as educated as they are, or as knowledgeable as they are. Some use their insider knowledge to their profit and cheat their organization and those about them. That is, they do anything that gives the impression that they are more successful than their competition. Such was the case of King Saul, who was very weak in character. His is rise to power made him worse than he ever might have been.

Yes, the corruption of leadership comes in many forms - whether it is listening to the flattery of people, or it is deceit and conceit, or in lying and stealing, or in coveting or what have you - leadership offers many opportunities to be corrupted.

Anyone of us who think of ourselves as leaders needs to take caution because the opportunity that is presented to any one person to be corrupted is opened to all of us. So all of us need to check ourselves often to see that we are not being damaged.

THE COST OF LEADERSHIP

We often hear the reference, "If you cannot take the heat, get out of the kitchen." It is quite applicable for any who seek to lead, for there is a very high price to pay. I do not wish to scare anyone who is called or tries to lead, for a world without leaders would be a world that is lost. People need leadership. And somebody must direct. But, without any apology, leadership cost.

Ask Moses; he sensed the cost from the moment that God met him at the burning bush. That is why he sought to make so many excuses. Among the excuses, he wanted God to remember that he had a stuttering tongue. "O my Lord, I *am* not eloquent, neither before nor since You have spoken to Your servant, but I *am* slow of speech and slow of tongue." (Exodus 4:10, 11 NKJV). But God saw in him gifts that only a few mortals possess and offered him multiple encouragements. He finally relented and accepted that there was a task to do, to help take him people out of oppression. Along the way to Egypt and on reaching Egypt he was to meet many frustrations. His encounters with Pharaoh were more than many mortals could take. When he left Egypt and came to the Red Sea, with some two million people, with their many complaints, for fear of the Egyptian army in pursuit, he cried out to God and God told him to lift his rod and hold it up to the Sea. The waters parted for Israel to cross over on dry ground. After crossing the Red Sea, in their forty years of travel through the wilderness, the people complained often. For example, when Moses went up to Mount Sinai to receive the tablets of the Ten Commandments, the people turned to the worship of the Golden Calf. On seeing and hearing the rebellion in the camp, Moses broke the tables of the Ten Commandments. On another occasion, as the people complained about thirst, God told Moses to speak to a rock to get water. The cry of the people was so great that Moses to strike the rock. On another occasion when the people had become so rebellious that God decided to wipe them out from the face of the earth, Moses pleaded with God and requested God to take his own life instead of the people's. At the end of the wilderness journey, Moses was not permitted to enter the earthly Canaan land. He was only permitted to look at the land from the top of Pisgah. His was a life of service, sacrifice, and suffering. The writer of Hebrews reflects on his life thus, "He chose to suffer affliction with the people of God than to enjoy the pleasures of sin for a season." (Hebrews 11).

Thank God that God had a big plan for Moses as he has for the rest of us who are willing to offer our lives service, sacrifice, suffering as leaders, like Moses. I use Moses as a paradigmatic example, but leadership that is effective in any context, sacred and secular is demanding. As we said, "Uneasy is the head that wears a crown?" Do I need to speak of the quintessential example of service, sacrifice, and suffering? I think not, for not everyone will have to serve, or sacrifice, or suffer in the same way like Moses or Jesus, or the Apostle Paul or Augustine, or Martin Luther or Martin Luther King Jr. or Robert F. Kennedy, or some of the other great examples that I could quote from Scripture or extra biblical sources. Yes, not everyone might have to bear the same cost, but where ever one seeks to lead in a practical way, leaderships cost.

Instead of detailing the costs of the service, sacrifice, and suffering, I only ask how effective do you want to be a leader? How much are you willing to pay to make your leadership effective? I have said this often, but need to repeat it, leadership is not about power, or position, or popularity as it is about service, sacrifice, and suffering. Still, are you prepared to pay the cost?

ASSESSING HOW YOU LEAD

In one of the institutions I worked, for many years, we had to do self-evaluations, collegial assessments, departmental assessments, and sometimes formal assessments according to top administrative demands. It seemed a lot of pressure at the times of the years when the assessments had to be done. Those of us who took the estimates seriously prepared ourselves for them and sought to be efficient and effective in our work. We also tried to maintain good graces with those who came to assess us. Our portfolios were in place and we prepared to answer demanding questions that we imagined would be posed to us. Although we were assured that the intent of the assessments was to help us grow, at times we felt that they were quite intimidating.

Some of us asked, on occasion, "Do we really have to do these assessments?" But whether we liked it or not, we had to do them, if we wanted to keep our jobs. Of course, one needs not think that our institution was stricter than others. To a greater or lesser degree, leaders are constantly being assessed. And although we might not call out loudly like the old New York City Mayor, Eduard Koch, "How am I doing?" yet we know that we are being assessed. In fact, if at all you are a leader of any sort, ask yourself the following questions:

1. Do you love what you are doing?
2. Do you know the depth of your commitment to what you are doing?

3. Are you willing to acknowledge your strengths and weaknesses?
4. Do you have a high quality of respect for others?
5. Do you seek to build people up or tear them down?
6. Do you accept the criticism of others as a way to grow?
7. Do you ask others what you can do better in your leadership position?
8. Do you like to praise others for their outstanding contributions to what you are seeking to accomplish?
9. Do you like to surround yourself with people who are gifted, even above yourself?
10. Are you a traditionalist or are you willing to accommodate new ways of thinking?
11. Are you a transactionalist – a maintenance leader or are you a transformationalist - an agent of change?
12. Are you a visionary or a pragmatist – one who just see things as they are?
13. Do you seek to develop the potential in those about you or do you discourage talent and gift development?
14. How do you approach challenges, fearfully or faithfully?
15. How do you approach opportunities?
16. Are you a trust builder of a trust-buster?
17. Are you a truth teller or do you like to spread "fake news"?
18. Are you a good listener or do you just like to babble on and on?
19. Do you have leadership a vision for what you seek to accomplish?

20. Do you seek leadership because of what you can gain, or what you can give?

These are just a few of the assessment questions that every leader should ask himself/herself. Our effectiveness depends on our seriousness in responding to the questions. Only with such kind of assessment could the Apostle Paul come to the end of his life and says, "I have fought a good fight, I have finished my course, I have kept the faith."

THE GREATEST TEMPTATIONS OF LEADERSHIP

After preaching at my mother-in-law's memorial service, a lot of people came up to me, while others called to say, "You out-preached yourself - this is the greatest sermon I have heard you preach." Yes, my mother-in-law and I were great friends. However, while I was gratified that people did not call up to say that I blew it, I am not so foolish to accept the compliment in the way that they have stated it. I am happy that the sermon went well. It was intended to be, but it pushed me to think more about the topic on which I had been reflecting over the last few days - "the temptations of leadership." It is so easy to get distracted and fall into temptations of the flesh, such as accepting the praise of people and getting caught in self-adulation. No place is easier to face the kind of temptations that I am thinking of than in leadership. We all face temptations in our different spheres, some more than others, but the saying is true, "The higher the monkey climbs, the more he is exposed."

When one leads, one has to be aware that, one will often face all kinds of temptations. Patrick Lencioni, in his popular bestseller, *The Five Temptations of the CEO*, names them as: 1. Status over results. 2. Popularity over accountability. 3. Certainty over clarity. 4. Harmony over conflict. 5. Invulnerability over trust. I wish I had time to comment on each of the five, for they are profoundly relevant, but hopefully they are self-explanatory. I want to add another twelve to his list, that I call the constants:

1. The use and misuse of power
2. Taking credit for the successes of others
3. Blaming and projecting on others for one's personal mistakes
4. Over-busyness in fulfilling a role with the prospect of burnout
5. Self-reliance and self-dependence
6. Forgetting personal development
7. Forgetting self-assessment for self-improvement
8. Turf protection
9. Failure to discern – an unwillingness to admit blind spots
10. Neglect of spiritual time
11. Failure to take advise
12. Being overcome by frustrations

There are indeed more than we can list, but suffice it to say, the devil has a barrel of temptations waiting to bring out for anyone who is willing to be an effective leader. He brought them to Jesus Christ (cf. Matthew 4), so who are we to think that we are exempt? The devil just needs to find the suited personality, occasion, and condition to bring out the temptations. Some of us even blame God for our temptations. We like to blame everything on the devil, or even on God. But more often than not, our temptations come from within. Our passions, our habits, and our characters get us into trouble. The apostle James says, "When tempted, no one should say, "God is tempting me." For God cannot be tempted by evil, nor does he tempt anyone; but each person is tempted when they are dragged away by their own evil desire and enticed. Then, after desire has conceived, it gives birth to sin; and sin, when it is full-grown, gives birth to death." (James 1:13-15 NIV).

In effect, to be successful in leadership one needs to understand the power of temptations. One needs to realize that temptations are intended to degrade our character, destroy our physical well-being, destroy our spiritual lives, break down our whole humanity, and eliminate whatever successes we might have in life. When we yield to temptations we are on the path of degradation and destruction. It is therefore essential for us to accept what Jesus said to his disciples, "Watch and pray so that you will not fall into temptation." Understanding that "the spirit is willing but the flesh is weak." (Matthew 26:41).

THE CREDIBILITY OF LEADERSHIP

The concept of credibility in leadership is receiving considerable attention with the confirmation hearings for Judge Brett Michael Kavanaugh to the Supreme Court of the United States. The haste with which he was to be voted by the Judiciary Committee and the Senate is on hold, at least for a little while. The ongoing debate is that there needs to be clarification on the accusation of sexual harassment/assault that has been brought against the Judge by a woman. He has flatly denied any contact with the woman, but she is insistent that he attacked her while they were in their teens. Whose word is credible, is the question to be resolved.

In the present political climate, credibility might not make a significant difference, because while one side is saying it does matter, the other hand has already made up their minds about whose side they are on. All that is being done is defending or intimidating one each other by shouting the loudest, to see who will win in the confirmation.

But when the dust settles, people will have to return to the question of whether credibility makes a difference in leadership. And whether they like it or not they will have to admit, from deep in their hearts, that it matters, for it impacts, loyalty, commitment, energy, and productivity. Over the long haul, credibility will not be decided by a political victory, but by morality. Morality is something that God has placed in the human heart, and whether we like it or not, we make judgments and declare our loyalty and commitment, on the basis of whether we trust the credibility of the other.

Credibility is called "the foundation of leadership." Thus, whether one likes it or not, people use it to make their judgment on their long-term connection to a leader. When they check out the qualities of any leader, they want to know how competent is the leader. But beyond competence in the long term, they will seek to focus on the character and conduct of the leader. Is the leader honest? Is the leader truthful? Is the leader consistent? Is the leader authentic? Is the leader transparent? Does the leader care? Other things might be added as one makes a judgment on the credibility of the leader, for credibility is more complicated than the simplistic ways in which it is often presented in the political sphere.

Credibility is to be view in long-term relationships. People might meet an individual and they claim that they find with such a one a natural synergy, and instantly they begin to bond. At such a point, communication and the building of a foundation of a relationship start smoothly, however in the long term, the synergy will wear away, if the person is inconsistent and untrustworthy. Yes, credibility is to be viewed in the long run. And people will break apart and seek relationships with the ones they can trust.

The point is that we all need to learn that we must live our lives with credibility. Jesus said, "Let your yes be yes, and your no be no." (Matthew 5:37). The Apostle Paul said, "Let your speech be always gracious, seasoned with grace so that you can have the right response from everyone." (Colossians 4:6). Not only our words, but every action, not just when we rise to be leaders in high positions, but along the road of our lives we need to make our every word and action be underlined by credibility. As we contemplate the likelihood of those about us, let us ask ourselves, how credible are we?

THE EFFECTIVENESS OF LEADERSHIP

We are living in an exciting time. One in which the president of the United States is making the claim that he is the most effective president since the last 50 years or more. In listening to him, I have gone back to check the accomplishments of some others, and asked what does he mean by being the most effective? What does it say to be an effective leader? Does it mean one who is inspirational rather than transformational? Or what? The president ran a campaign on being transformational, and one cannot say that he has not fulfilled some of the goals and objectives that he set forth to achieve. He likely has turned back the hands of the clock in many aspects that others might have considered forward progress, but questions are still being raised on his effectiveness.

Of course, my reflection is not intended to make a judgment on the president of the United States, but to allow each of us to ask ourselves how effective have we been as leaders in our different spheres. As parents how successful have we been with our children? As pastors how constructive in our churches? As teachers how effective have we been in our classrooms? For me, effectiveness means more than achieving a list of immediate goals and objectives. It means more than production. When I think of effectiveness, I reflect on a leader's moral influence on a community or organization. How positively transforming is such a leader? To bring the question near to our hearts, we might ask about personages such as Hitler, Mussolini, Pol

Pot, and other brutal characters of the world? How effective have they been? How well have their leadership resulted in the positive development of people's lives or how much have their work diminished people's lives? How healthy have they displayed integrity? In what ways have they been positively transformative for generations to come?

If my examples seem harsh, pardon me, but it is my wish that we turn the searchlight on ourselves? How effective have we been? Are we more conscious of production instead of personal transformation? A Chinese proverb that challenged my reflection states, "He who sacrifices his conscience to gain ambition burns a picture to obtain ashes." I am afraid that too many persons in our world today are fooled by the shadows of success and fail to be effective in the long term. They are fooled by immediate material achievements and fail to live to the glory of God. As the Apostle Paul rightly instructs, ". . . whatever you do, do it all for the glory of God." (1 Corinthians 10:31).

It is a great temptation for leaders to focus on themselves and their accomplishments rather than the giving of glory to God. Think of great characters like Moses, David, Nehemiah, Jesus and the Apostle Paul, did they not face such temptations? There were multiple ways in which Satan sought to make them ineffective, but they were able to overcome him, by humbling themselves before God.

To be most effective we need to learn how to follow the way of God. He will make us more effective by making up where we fall short in our leadership performance.

THE ACCOUNTABILITY OF LEADERSHIP

If there is anything that the Me Too Movement has taught us, it is that men, even in high positions of leadership, can be held accountable for the sins of youth or the power plays of manhood. A lot that has been done in secret is coming into the open. Many leaders have had to resign from their leadership of organizations, others have been removed. Some of the most powerful men have been put in jail. In the many cases that have been prosecuted in the public courts, when the defendant is declared guilty and sentenced to prison, prosecutors are proclaiming that "Justice has been served." It is pathetic that the truth has to be squeezed out of so many who would like to make others responsible for their misdeeds.

Now, while it is tough to prove the truth or falsehood against all the men who have been accused, enough men have fallen from their positions of power by the allegations to say that the effort of the women to call the men to accountability has proven effective. After first denying their behavior many men are being forced to accept that the best way to deal with their situation is to get out of the way.

Of course, we should not think that accountability is only connected to sexual matters, for accountability crosses every sphere of our lives. It impacts our relationships and our governance in our homes, in our churches and in the public areas. It influences our social perceptions and consumer preferences. It tells people about the kinds of attitudes they might have toward an organization one leads. These days the news media, and the movie industry are being called to accountability.

In reality, the call for accountability is not a contemporary requirement, but as old as the creation itself. From the beginning of time, God has given to humanity moral sensitivity to make us accountable. Remember the story, when God created Adam and Eve, he told them, "Of every tree of the garden you may freely eat; but of the tree of the knowledge of good and evil you shall not eat, for in the day that you eat of it you shall surely die." (Genesis 2:16, 17 NKJV). Not long after their placement in the Garden of Eden, Adam and Eve were tested and miserably failed the test, by listening to the serpent. The story is told that "the serpent was more cunning than any beast of the field which the Lord God had made. And he said to the woman, "Has God indeed said, 'You shall not eat of every tree of the garden'?" 2 And the woman said to the serpent, "We may eat the fruit of the trees of the garden; 3 but of the fruit of the tree which *is* in the midst of the garden, God has said, 'You shall not eat it, nor shall you touch it, lest you die.'" 4 Then the serpent said to the woman, "You will not surely die. 5 For God knows that in the day you eat of it your eyes will be opened, and you will be like God, knowing good and evil." 6 So when the woman saw that the tree *was* good for food, that it *was* pleasant to the eyes, and a tree desirable to make *one* wise, she took of its fruit and ate. She also gave to her husband with her, and he ate. 7 Then the eyes of both of them were opened, and they knew that they *were* naked, and they sewed fig leaves together and made themselves coverings." (Genesis 3:1-7 NKJV).

The point is that when one disdains what God says, and listens to the serpent, and even lies to oneself, about his or her accountability, such an individual will ultimately find that he/she will have to confess the truth to God. All the effort to avoid responsibility will not suffice, for the responsibility that we fail to accept in the here and now we will be called to receive at the judgment seat of Christ, where "every knee shall bow, and every tongue shall confess that Jesus Christ is Lord." (Romans 14:10, 11).

In whatever we do, let us practice be responsible now, even if it is just getting a friend to call us to accountability.

LEADING IN THE AGE OF NEW MEDIA

President Donald Trump has mastered the art of using Twitter to influence the minds of a majority of Americans. Even those who think he is their "enemy number one," are often fixated on his announcements made by tweets. It is said that he has over 55,000,000 contacts in his tweet accounts. And since becoming president, his tweet counter notes that he has produced over 30,000 tweets. He has both personal and official tweet accounts. And he uses the tweets, to announce and control the news of the day, such as what he thinks of opponents. He tweets of those he wishes to hire, and those he wishes to fire. He also uses his tweets to call out, what he names Fake News, attacks varied media organizations, express his pride of achievements, and defends himself against any potential negative charge. If one should ask, how is Mr. Trump's presidency different from all others? One would have to answer, he tweets. He uses it for rapid response to the news of the day. It is argued that he has a greater grasp of the power of media in the modern technological frame, than all the presidents before him. He knows how to use them for attraction or distraction. If he does not feel that the media is benefiting his purposes he knows how to attack it and dispose of it.

My point for using President Trump's use of the contemporary media, as my point of departure, was not to state how much I admire him, or stand on the side of the political platform against Mr. Trump.

My point is to argue that as a leader in the contemporary culture, he understands the power of media and how to use it for his advantage. The greater point is that anyone who seeks to be effective needs to understand the media, and use it to seek the good of those being led. Among the media that need our greatest attention is, Google, Facebook, Instagram, Twitter, emails, streaming, YouTube, radio, and TV. These are all part and parcel of the contemporary media that a leader must affirm or disaffirm. They are among the media that have the most powerful influence in the culture in which we research and share information, facilitate communication, administer power and authority, make decisions and find opportunities to transform and grow the organizations or communities in which we lead.

Anyone who understands the legacy of leadership for the next generation, must adjust to the transformative nature of contemporary media. Those who show resistance are bound to fail. The failure of Kodak is an example of a company that failed to adjust from an analog to a digital age. The institution where I taught and held administrative responsibilities came up with one of the earliest Adult Degree (Education) Program(s) in the United States of America, but I watched in its time of struggle, and its failure to change. Along with our then president, a few of us were fighting for the transformation, but we were outvoted. A couple of us, even did alternative additional terminal degrees to find out how to create the change that was needed. But the model of paper and attendance on campus were seen by the majority of faculty as so sacred, that there was no push to change. After 25 years of success, the mode of the program delivery became outmoded and folded, along with the rest of the college. Of course, what is described is not so unique, multiple examples across organizations, institutions and corporations can be cited that have gone to their quiet home. As was stated, some who led sought to change, but the organizational or community cultures were so resistant, the organizations or communities folded. More often than not, it is the leaders who fail to adopt to the rapid transformation and therefore led the failure.

Having spoken of the need to adjust, affirm and adopt the contemporary media, one should not be blind to the fact that there are profound challenges that are to be dealt with, in the use of such media. For example, one needs to be aware of the need for the protection of privacy and obtaining security. It is also known that easy access to the greatest volume of information that this world has ever known, has been overwhelming and confusing. That means one needs guidance and wisdom in how the volume of information is used. Questions such as, where is the information from? How authentic is it? Is it true or is it false (Fake)? Who is it seeking to influence? Does it seek to build up people or tear them down? Does it seek to spread hatred and anger or outrage? Is it seeking to create peace or build battle lines? Does it engage in hyperbole, insults, shame and profanity? How balanced is it? Are all questions to be raised.

Yes, while we need to understand the power of contemporary media, and use them to facilitate the way we lead, we also need to understand their cautions. We need to learn from the creators of many of these media the potential for destruction of our organization, community, relationships and our total ways of positive living. The story of Facebook with Mark Zuckerberg has been told in the US Congress. When he and his co-founder created Facebook, they did not understand its all-encompassing reach, and only now are they confessing their ignorance and the opportunities they provide for personal and social destruction.

As a Christian leader who affirm the contemporary media, I also sense my own need to take caution. This is why I turn to Scripture to find principles for how I go about the use. My first caution comes from the biblical prophet, Hosea, when he says concerning the destruction of Israel, "… My people are destroyed from lack of knowledge. Because you have rejected knowledge. . ." (Hosea 4:6, fp). Further, I take the caution from the Psalmist that we must be careful about over-trusting all human development. In the words of the Psalmist, "Some trust in chariots and some in horses, but we trust in the name of the LORD our God." (Psalm 20:7). That is, we must never let pride in the developments take away our ethical responsibility. Additionally, we need to be aware of the use of our language, especially when we are not face to face with one another. What the apostle James says in a more traditional context has relevance here, namely: "With the tongue we praise our Lord and Father, and with it we curse human beings, who have been made in God's likeness (James 3:9). The apostle Paul put it another way, "Do not let any unwholesome talk come out of your mouths, but only what is helpful for building others up according to their needs, that it may benefit those who listen. [30] And do not grieve the Holy Spirit of

God, with whom you were sealed for the day of redemption. [31] Get rid of all bitterness, rage and anger, brawling and slander, along with every form of malice. [32] Be kind and compassionate to one another, forgiving each other, just as in Christ God forgave you." (Ephesians 4:29-32 NIV).

Much more could be said, but it is my estimation that, the point is clear that contemporary media (of every form) needs to be affirmed, adopted and assessed in our effort to make most positive and effective our leadership today. We must be constantly aware that the new media provide avenues to create the most extensive legacies that has ever been created in history. Therefore, let us be careful to use them with discipline, dignity and decency.

THE CELEBRATION OF LEADERSHIP

It is of interest to me, when I hear various political leaders today, with their boast of accomplishments, how little praise they give to those about them. It is especially fascinating when the current president of the United States stands in the Rose Garden of the White House and calls a news conference to announce, with what is termed hyperbolical statements, his accomplishments in the rise of the stock market, the lowering of unemployment, trade, and tariffs and so on; and of course, his claims that no president in the last 50 to 100 years has accomplished as much as he has in such a short time.

Sometimes, when I hear the president, I have muttered that it sounds a lot like Nebuchadnezzar the king of Babylon who walked on the wall of the city and exclaimed, "Is not this the great Babylon I have built as the royal residence, by my mighty power and for the glory of my majesty!" (Daniel 4:31 NIV). While I'm not using this reflection to caution the president, for I do not know that he would take time to read what is said here, it is important to use what follows Nebuchadnezzar's exclamation as a caution for all of us. The story states: "Even as the words were on his lips, a voice came from heaven, 'This is what is decreed for you, King Nebuchadnezzar: Your royal authority has been taken from you. You will be driven away from people and will live with the wild animals; you will eat grass like the ox. Seven times will pass by for you until you acknowledge that the Most High is sovereign over all kingdoms on earth and gives them to anyone he wishes.' Immediately what had been said about Nebuchadnezzar was fulfilled. He was driven away from people and ate grass like the ox. His body was drenched with the dew of heaven until his hair grew like the feathers of an eagle and his nails like the claws of a bird." (Daniel 4:32-33 NIV).

What humiliation? My point is to take note that what the current president and Nebuchadnezzar have done in the extreme, is a problem that is very common in the culture of leadership in public and private establishments. There is that tendency to take credit to one's self for what has been accomplished by so many others. One might find this tendency even in churches - a minister taking credit for members that have been added to a congregation as if it were done by himself/herself alone. Yes, there is a great temptation to self-aggrandize.

Of course, such caution and the possibility of a divine judgment as I have noted above does not say that we are not to celebrate leadership; leaders need to celebrate and be celebrated. Leaders need to take time to give credit for what has been accomplished through them and those about them, with the help of God. We all need to remember that much of what is achieved in life is through team effort, instead of by any one person.

In effect, leadership celebration needs to recognize the contributions, assistance, sacrifice, help, service, creativity, support, cooperation, et cetera of others. Leadership celebration needs to be done humbly and selflessly. It is not a time for boasting proudly and strutting around ostentatiously, but instead, a time for recognizing what has been done together through the help of God. We should not forget that God knows the truth of all we have accomplished. This is why Jesus lays out God's final evaluation of how a master commended his servants:

> His lord said to him, 'Well done, good and faithful servant; you were faithful over a few things, I will make you ruler over many things. Enter into the joy of your lord.' 22 He also who had received two talents came and said, 'Lord, you delivered to me two talents; look, I have gained two more talents besides them.' 23 His lord said to him, 'Well done, good and faithful servant; you have been faithful over a few things, I will make you ruler over many things. Enter into the joy of your lord' (Matthew 25:21-23 (NKJV).

As you take time to celebrate your leadership; whether in your home, family, church, community or in public life, think of what the Lord thinks of you. Give him praise for his blessings. And do not forget those about you who have helped you along the way. Remember that you do not lead alone. As is said, if you want to know how effective a leader you are, look behind you who is following you.

MAKING A DIFFERENCE IN LEADERSHIP

The topic "Making a difference in leadership" is a profoundly interesting one. It leads to the thought that a great many persons come on the scene of action and seem to make very little difference with their lives. They enter the world with great expectations, but leave the world with no legacy at all. If you go to their funerals you will hear testimonials, and wonder what have they accomplished. Often people try to "make up stuff" to so that there will be the appearance of their effectiveness. But then you ask, what truly have they done. Yes, they might have created waves, but with very little impact. They create tremors but no quakes. Their contribution to life seems negligible. Their influence seems feeble. Their effect seems pitiable. They have moved along through the rung of life and soon after their passing, nobody remembers that they ever existed.

In thinking about the topic, the lives of the judges of Israel have been very appealing to me. The judges ruled for a period of time that most scholars say was about 325 to 388 years (beginning in app. 1400 - 1012 B.C.). Their rise and fall tell a lot about their own weaknesses and the patience of the divine. Through their lives are also given clues as to how God works with diverse personalities to accomplish his work. It is also notable that God is not tied to a gender but is willing to use male or female to accomplish what needs to be accomplished. When a person is submissive to the divine such a person can be used in a mighty way by God. Such a person can also be used to empower others.

Take a careful look at the chart that follows and note the differing levels of accomplishments by each judge. It is evident that not everyone made a great difference with their lives and the history of Israel. Take note of the scriptural record of their biography:

Name	Ruled	Text	Defining Action	Impact
Othniel	40 Years	Judges 3:7-11	Son of Kenaz, became the son –in-law of Caleb. After Chushan-rishathaim, the king of Aram-Naharaim, oppressed the people of Debir for eight years; when they "cried" unto God, **Othniel was** raised up to be their deliverer. And under him peace lasted for forty years.	**High**
Ehud	40 Years		Ehud, the left-handed judge, who delivered Israel from the hands of the Moabites	**Moderate**
Shamgar	10 Years	Judges 3:31	Repelled the Philistine incursion into Israelite Territory. Slaughtered 600 invaders with an ox goad.	**Moderate**
Deborah and	40 Years	Judges 4; 5	Prophetess and judge of Israel who told Barak that	**High**

Barak			God was sending him to lead a military expedition against Jabin the king of the Canaanites and Sisera his commander. Barak was so cold-footed that Deborah had to help lead the army. After the victory Judges records one of the most powerful victory song in the Bible, to celebrate the work of Deborah.	
Gideon – also called Jerubbaal	40 Years	Judges 3:31	Military leader, Judge and Prophet Led Israel in battle against the Midianites He won a decisive military victory with only 300 soldiers. We talk often of power of Gideon's army – recognizing it as the intervention of God.	High
Tola	23 Years	Judges 4; 5	Lived at Shamir in Mount Ephraim.	Low
Jair (Yair)	22 Years	Judges 10:3-5	Was the son of Machir. Had 30 sons who rode on colts and controlled 30 cities.	Low

THE LEGACY OF LEADERSHIP

Jephthah	6 years	Judges 11:1-12:7	Father a Gileadite, mother a prostitute. Went to war against the Philistines and defeated them.	Moderate
Ibzan	7 Years	Judges 12:8-10	Had 30 sons and 30 daughters. Sent abroad for wives for his sons	Low
Elon	10 Years	Judges 12:13-15	Had 40 sons and 30 grandsons. Believed to have been wealthy since he provided donkeys for his sons and grandsons.	Low
Abdon	8 Years	Judges 12:13-15	Was buried in the hill country of the Amalekites.	Very Low
Eli	40 Years	1 Samuel 1:1-3-6:22	Eli was the judge of Israel that succeeded Samson. He was High Priest in Shiloh. His story is profoundly interesting, because by the time he became priest, the spiritual life of Israel had been profoundly depreated and he did little to turn it back in a positive direction. he seemed to have been a good caregiver for Samuel, he was a very weak and negligent father. He did not seriously challenge his sons when they practiced all the wickedness they did in the	Moderate And Negative

			sanctuary of God. As such he set the basis for the "glory of God" (the Ark) to be taken from Israel. When the news came to him that the Ark of God was captured by the Philistines, he fell off a wall at the tabernacle gate and died.	
Samson	Judges 13:1- 16:31	20 Years	Samson was a miracle baby whose parents was told that they should grow him up as a Nazarite. However, because through his life he constantly made false choices, he got into trouble, but God continued to use him anyway. He did fantastic things such as killing a lion (Judges 14:5-6), tying 300 foxes together a burning down the fields in a Philistine village (Judges 15:4), and allowing himself to be tied with strong ropes as if to be captured, but when the Philistines came to take him he broke the cords (Judges 15:13-14), and picking up the iron gate of Gaza and taking it 30 miles	**Moderate And Negative**

			away when the citizens secured the gated, so that he was not able to get out (Judges 16:2-3). Some acts of his life are to be called totally foolish, such as when he married the prostitute of Surek, and when he married Delilah which lead him to give away the secrets of his strength which lead to his imprisonment and death.	
			His greatest contribution to the Judgeship of Israel came when he went to war against the Philistines and killed a thousand of them. Then at his death he was able to shake the columns of Dagan's temple, thus taking the lives of 1000s of Philistines.	
Samuel	1 Samuel and 2 Samuel	77 years began at age 13 and continued until he was 90.	Samuel was a miracle child, given to his mother Hannah in answer to prayer. His name means "God has heard." He was a judge, priest, and prophet. He was the king-maker who anointed Saul and David. He became a reformer of the faith of Israel, who set up the	**A profound impact. He truly made a great and positive difference**

schools of the prophets. Led Israel in battle against the Philistines at Mizpah to secure the Ark of God.

His two sons, Joel and Abijah were a disappointment as they followed the very corrupt ways of the sons of Eli. This led to the transition from the judgeship to the kingship.

In his farewell speech he warned Israel that they would regret choosing a king. He also reminded them that they were to give up their idols and serve the true and the living God.

Because his sons did not follow in his footsteps the people of Israel demanded a king.

So Samuel anointed Saul, as the first king of Israel, and David as the second king. Samuel was not afraid to bring counsel or criticism to king Saul.

His two sons, Joel and Abijah were a

			disappointment as they followed the very corrupt ways of the sons of Eli. This led to the transition from the judgeship to the kingship.	
			In his farewell speech he warned Israel that they would regret choosing a king. He also reminded them that they were to give up their idols and serve the true and the living God.	

After reviewing these lives as I have done, let's take note of twenty things that have made those who had the greatest impact leaders with most effective legacy.

1. They are distinctive. They stand outside of the crowd. Those who cannot stand out from the crowd of ordinary people will not make a great different. This fact has been clear in every age. When God calls his people "a royal priesthood people," "a chosen people," "a holy people" "a people of his own making," "his servants" "a peculiar people" this is the point. They are God dependent. They recognize that they need to be God, dependent. They are distinctly different from everybody else. They work for God and not just for men or women. They work for God and not just for government, a school system, a church, or some other industry.

2. They live principled lives – They stand for something. They are people with integrity. They have a purpose. They are driven by a mission. They do not allow obstacles to destroy their dreams. They are faithful to the high trust that God has placed on them.
3. They are focused - not easily distracted –They say like the Apostle Paul did, "This one thing I do, forgetting the things that are behind and reaching for the things that are before. I press towards the mark of the high calling of God in Christ Jesus my Lord." (Philippians 3:13, 14). Or like Jesus, "For I have come down from heaven not to do my own will, but the will of the one that sent me." (John 6:38). "He went a little farther and fell on His face, and prayed, saying, "O My Father, if it is possible, let this cup pass from Me; nevertheless, not as I will, but as You *will*." *(Matthew 26:39 NKJV)*.
4. They are other-centered – They are not turned in upon themselves. They are unselfish. They are self-giving. They constantly seek to bless others. Like the poem attributed to Charles D. Meigs (written between 1890 and 1902) says:

> Lord help me live from day to day in such a self-forgetful way that even when I kneel to pray My prayer shall be for – Others.
>
> Help me in all the work I do to ever be sincere and true and know that all I do for you Must needs be done for – Others.

> Let "Self" be crucified and slain and buried deep; and all in vain May efforts be to rise again Unless to live for – Others.
>
> And when my work on earth is done and my new work in heaven's begun May I forget the crown I've won While thinking still of – Others.
>
> Others, Lord, yes others Let this my motto be Help me to live for others That I may live like Thee.

5. They take initiative. They do not sit down and wait for things to happen to them or around them. They stay on the offensive. They know how and when to use defense. They act instead of react.

6. They are responsive to change – They recognize that doing the same thing in the same way, all the time is foolish, and the path to failure. That is, they constantly monitor their environment for the strategy that suits the time. Samuel, realized that there was moral degradation in Israel and went about setting up the schools of the prophets. When prophet Elijah came on the scene of action, he recognized that the schools had fallen into apostasy, and went about reforming them. He was constant or diligent in his effort, and God blessed him.

7. They are creative – If they do not have a sword they will use "the jaw-bone of an ass," as in the case of Samson, or "a sling and a small stone," as David did as he approached the giant Goliath.

8. They are disciplined stewards. They do not waste time, energy or money. They do not squander resources. They do not hoard.
9. They are decisive (versus being indecisive). They make decisions. They stick to that which they have decided, but are not inflexible or intransigent. They are not like Jephthah who made the foolish vow and would not change, thus losing his daughter. When they are given reasons to change they change.
10. They are wise (and discerning). They take time to contemplate. They have a clear sense of perception. They know how to use their judgment. In the sample of judges that leaders we have presented as leaders, it is clear that not all were wise. Samson was powerful and strong, but in matters that demanded wisdom, he was puerile. We might say the same of Jephthah and Eli, they lacked the kind of wisdom that is desirable in judgeship.
11. They have a clear sense of justice. The judges of Israel we called because they had to lead armies against nations that sought to oppress Israel, however we are not to think that justice is only needed against outside enemies. In just about every context of life, here are in-equitabilities that need attention. Legacy minded leaders are called to ameliorate such in-equitabilities.
12. They are incarnational leaders. They have the ability to connect with those they lead. One cannot be an effective leader if one is an isolationist. Neither can one be successful

if one stands above other, look down on others, despise others. I have heard it said by a leader, "I like what I am doing except for the people." How can that be? When one leads, one is leading people

13. They understand the world of competition. Like it or not, no one is able to live effectively without facing the competing forces in the world. There are competing principles and values. In the context in which we write, we take note that there is competition between the church and other non-profit organizations in the world. There is, for example, competition between Christian and other forms of education. There is competition between the word of God and the word of the serpent. As the apostle Paul says, "we wrestle not against flesh and blood, but against principalities, against powers, high places." (Ephesians 6:12 KJV). Competition is the reality of the world, and for we are wrestling against the rulers of the darkness of this world, against spiritual wickedness in while some of us do not like the term, we cannot avoid it and must use it to win in the battles of life.

14. They are willing to work hard – Being diligent and persistent. They are not lazy, mentally or otherwise. They develop themselves. They sharpen their skills, multiply their gifts, improve their talents. And seek to accomplish with excellence the tasks that stands before them.

15. They are driven – When they are challenged they are do not become distracted. They are intensely focused on their purpose. They keep their goal before and will make great

sacrifices to attain it. From the list of the judges we have named, I opine that Othniel, Gideon, Jephthah, Deborah and Samuel were the most driven. They faced the challenges that came to them fearlessly. They were persistent and thus were able to energize and mobilize others to join them.

16. They seek to identify and develop critical competency skills – When one is called to lead, it is crucial that one has certain competencies. However, it is even more important that a leader will seek to strengthen the competencies that the leader has been given. As is said, "Competencies are the best predictors of leadership success." Reflect on the following, for example and ask, which of the ten were in the judges that we named on the table.

    a. Analytical
    b. Communication
    c. Planning and organizing
    d. Management
    e. Multi-tasking
    f. Prioritizing
    g. Adaptability/flexibility
    h. Decision making
    i. Conflict management
    j. Interpersonal relationships

These and more are crucial competencies that are found is the best of leaders through the ages.

17. They understand timing – As is said, "Timing is everything." Such is the understanding of effective leaders. They respond to situations in a timely manner. They understand that leaders who have gotten their timing wrong have failed. Those who go to war understand timing. They know that if they miss the timing their army will be defeated. In industry timing is crucial. If leaders fail to change at appropriate times, they will be left behind. Yes, timing makes the difference between victory and defeat.

18. Thy know how to manage power – Those who lead have the ability to influence and exert authority over others. Thus, every leader need to ask themselves, how do they use power? Whether they are corrupted by power? Are they reasonable or unreasonable in their demands on others? Do they empower or exploit others? Do they care about people or who coarse people? Do they threaten or intimidate those they lead? Do they abuse people to secure their loyalty? Do they manipulate and oppress people? Do they abuse people - physically, psychologically, emotionally, sexually, financially or spiritually? These are questions for every leader who seeks to leave a positive legacy.

19. The have high sense of morality – How values, virtue and character impact one's leadership? In the world in which we find ourselves we need serious reflection on the question of leadership and morality, for sometimes it seems that money is more important than morality. But it is clear that lack of morality creates irresponsibility. It is notable that those who

exhibit a low standard of morality, diminished their capacity to be to gain the trust of those they lead. When they lead an organization, they may find support from those they lead, but it won't be long before the systems in which they lead face anxiety and destruction. Morality creates integrity. Integrity creates trust. And trust creates harmony. In effect, no matter how successful leadership might seem, without morality it will come to a place where it will self-destruct.

20. They mentor others – Mentoring is one of the greatest evidence that a person is a legacy type leader. Before on passes off the scene of action, one needs to ask what legacy am I leaving behind. In the relay of life who has taken the banner from me? Who has learned the principles and values for which the most effective human beings have stood through the centuries? A true reality of life is that success is long-term, not short term.

Allow me to ask about you personally, What have you done that has been transformational in leadership? What has been your accomplishments? What legacy are you leaving behind?

In his *Psalm of Life*, Henry Wadsworth Longfellow, tells us what the heart of a young man said to a Psalmist. It is my view that his Psalm (poem) has some bad theology but poses a realistic question, namely:

> Tell me not, in mournful numbers, Life is but an empty dream!

For the soul is dead that slumbers, and things are not what they seem.

Life is real! Life is earnest! And the grave is not its goal; Dust thou art, to dust returnest,

Was not spoken of the soul.

Not enjoyment, and not sorrow, Is our destined end or way;

But to act, that each to-morrow Find us farther than to-day.

Art is long, and Time is fleeting, And our hearts, though stout and brave,

Still, like muffled drums, are beating Funeral marches to the grave.

In the world's broad field of battle, In the bivouac of Life,

Be not like dumb, driven cattle! Be a hero in the strife!

Trust no Future, howe'er pleasant! Let the dead Past bury its dead!

Act,— act in the living Present! Heart within, and God o'erhead!

Lives of great men all remind us We can make our lives sublime,

And, departing, leave behind us Footprints on the sands of time;

Footprints, that perhaps another, Sailing o'er life's solemn main,

A forlorn and shipwrecked brother, Seeing, shall take heart again.

Let us, then, be up and doing, With a heart for any fate;

Still achieving, still pursuing, learn to labor and to wait.

After focusing as intensively as we have on the qualities that make for the legacy of leadership, we need to ask ourselves, when the time of our departure comes from this world, what will be said of the difference that our lives have made. Will we be able to say, like the Apostle Paul, "I have fought the good fight, I have finished the race, I have kept the faith. 8 Now there is in store for me the crown of righteousness, which the Lord, the righteous Judge, will award to me on that day—and not only to me, but also to all who have longed for his appearing. (2 Timothy 4:7, 8 NIV). Or like Jesus, "[Father] I have brought you glory on earth by finishing the work you gave me to do." (John 17:4 NIV).

We need not say more on the legacy of leadership, other than ask again, whether we have left a mark on the world that others will be able to follow?

PARENTING AND THE LEGACY OF LEADERSHIP

Any reflection on the legacy of leadership should include the impact of parents. Many organizations today are recognizing that the best way to find effective leaders is to teach parents how to be leaders. The assumptions are that:

1. Parents are the first leaders/teachers their children will ever see
2. Parents know their children best and understand the community in which their children reside.
3. Every parent has the potential to become a parent leader.
4. When parents lead, families will be strengthened.
5. Parents, in their fundamental role, shed a powerful influence as leaders.

My wife and I have been conducting parental legacy seminars and workshops for many years. Our interests began when we sought to reflect on our own family traditions and rituals. Aside from reviewing our traditions, we extended our reflections to our many friends and colleagues with whom we interacted. Specifically, we began to look at how they were parented, how they were parenting, and how, those not yet parents, plan to parent. This approach provided vital insights which we incorporated into our workshops and seminars. One workshop we conduct that gives us tremendous insights is *Parental*

Legacy. While we use multiple approaches in this particular workshop, we rely heavily on the use of worksheets where attendees really reflect on their upbringing and the impact it has on them. One expectation of this activity is that attendees become vulnerable in their responses. Most often as attendees work on the completing the assigned task, we watch carefully their body language and the questions they ask as they reflect on their great grandparents, grandparents, parents and the legacies passed on, or are passing to the next generation. Quite often, we see smiles, indicating some satisfaction with their response. However, we also note moments of frustration, confusion, sighs, deep groans and tears in some individuals, which indicate that they might be trying to deal with deep seated pain and hurt. Often as we ask for verbal answers, from those who are willing to share, a mix of emotions often come to the forefront. On quite a few occasions, we have had to wait patiently and allow people to share their joys or release their years of hurt and pain. Many times, some respondents not only want to talk about the legacy of blessings that their parents have given to them, but also the legacy of pain, anger, and resentment they carried over the years. On one occasion, we had to call for a therapist, for the pain and hurt for some were so deep that they needed immediate attention. What many came to find in the seminars and workshops is that the interconnections, positive or negative, between the generations are deeper than they sometimes knew or wished.

At times, many individuals desire to make a radical break with their parents and declare their individuality. However, they are often shocked by the reality of how much of the values and traditions of their parents they preserve and recycle. It does not take much scholarly research to confirm the continuity between one generation and another. So while there are vast differences between generations such as, Traditionalists (1900-1945), Baby Boomers (1946-1964), Generation X (1965-1980), Millennials (1981-2000) Generation Z, and all the contemporary generations identified, as they like to argue, there are many continuities that cannot be denied. People are not as unconnected from their roots as they would pretend or like to be. Some individuals might rebel, but what they come to find is that the interlinks are much stronger than they can shake off.

According to Dr. Jennifer J. Deal, a research scientist with the Center for Creative Leadership, the myth of generational differences withers as it comes face to face with the facts of the interconnections. She also notes that many social scientists are now admitting that the so-called generation gap is, in a large part, the result of miscommunication and misunderstanding, fueled by common insecurities and the desire for clout. She says that all generations have similar values. Noteworthy is the fact that family tops the list for all of the generations. It is in this context Deal lists the following as evidence of the interconnections.

- Everyone wants respect; however, the generations don't define it in the same way. Older individuals talk about respect in terms of "giving my opinions the weight I believe they deserve," while younger respondents characterize respect as "listen to me, pay attention to what I have to say."

- Leaders must be trustworthy. Different generations do not have notably different expectations of their leaders. Above all else, people of all ages want leaders they can trust.
- Nobody likes to change. The stereotype is that older people resist change while younger people embrace it. These assumptions don't stand up under the research, which found that people from all generations are uncomfortable with change. Resistance to change has nothing to do with age; it has to do with how much you stand to gain or lose as a result of the change.
- Loyalty depends on the context. Younger generations are not as loyal to their organizations as older workers. But the research shows, for example, that the amount of time a worker puts in each day has more to do with his or her status in the organization than with age. The higher the level, the more hours worked.
- Everyone wants to learn. Learning and development were among the issues brought up most frequently by people of all generations. Everyone wants to learn and to ensure they have the training to do their job well.
- Everyone likes feedback. According to the research, everyone wants to know how they are doing in order to learn how to do better.

What Deal says is entirely consistent with Scripture, which lays out the legacies of the kings of Israel in the North, and Judah in the South. Scripture shows much they followed their fathers, grandfathers or great grandfathers to do good or evil. Sometimes it was not a direct connection, but the legacies were manifested within the historical and familial lineage. For example, Scripture says, King "Baasha of Israel did evil in the sight of the Lord just like his father Jeroboam had done" (cf. 1 Kings 16:7). King "Ahab did evil in the sight of the Lord just as his father Omri had done" (1 Kings 16:30-31). King "Josiah of Judah did right in the sight of the Lord, just as his father David had done" (2 Kings 24:8, 9). King "Hezekiah did good in the eyes of the Lord, just as his father David hand done" (2 Chronicles 29:2). We could sight a host of other examples, but the fact is that whether intentionally or unintentionally, the legacies of these kings continued beyond their immediate lineage to the third and fourth generations.

According to a common saying, "The chip does not fall far from the block." Deny it, as people like to do, there is something about genes and socialization from which a person cannot run away. Also, the latter has much to do with how a leader is going to act and what attitude that leader will adopt. We might argue over individual responsibility versus corporate responsibility. We might say like the prophet Ezekiel, "Even if these three men, Noah, Daniel, and Job, were in it, they would deliver only themselves by their righteousness, says the Lord God" (Ezekiel 14:14 NKJV). We might point to the rebellion of children, as much as we want, the Word of God, and most social scientists are confident, that the patterns between parents and their children are consistent. The point is that leaders are much like those who parent them. Their vision, character, attitude, actions, effectiveness in decision making, discipline or lack of it, sense of responsibility, respect for truth, regard for people, respect for community, competences for relationship building, flexibility or rigidity, capacity for bonding, spirit of compassion, benevolence, proficiency with finance, creativity, work ethic, capacity for conflict management and other skills, are all impacted by how they were parented.

Here are some issues framed as questions to emphasize how parents might create legacies that impact leadership. One might not think of these in terms of the legacy of leadership, but can one afford to be uninformed about them?

USE OF AUTHORITY	The kind authority wielded in your home
	Is it authoritative?
	Is it authoritarian?
	Is it dogmatic?
	Is it permissive?
	Is it abusive?
	Is it benevolent?
INFLUENCE	The kind of influence on those at home
	Is it positive?
	Is it negative?
	Is it robust?
	Is it anemic?
	Is it life changing?
IMAGING OF THE DIVINE	When the divine is manifested through you
	Is the divine a character to be respected?
	Is the divine a character to be worshipped?
	Is the divine a character to be trusted?

	Is the divine an angry, transcendent character? Is the divine a loving and personal character?

ROLE MODELING	An effectiveness role-model in the home
	    Do you have time to serve others?
	    Do you always practice being positive, calm, and confident in whatever you do?
	    Are you very conscious that someone wants to follow you?

MENTORING	Measuring your mentorship
	    Do you think of what might be the possible outcomes of what you seek to do to those who are in your care?
	    How effective are you at motivating others to transform their behavior, without coercive actions?

ADVOCATING	Modeling how to do advocacy
	    Do you model before your children positive non-confrontational Advocacy?
	    Do they understand that advocacy does not mean?
	    destruction of resources or order?
	    That is does not disrespect cultural traditions and those who
	    who seek to maintain them?
	    Do they understand how to negotiate after failure?

CHANGE	How you as a parent adapt to change Are you flexible or inflexible?

	Have your parents ever contributed to any social changes that were taking place in your community? What impact did their contribution to the changes have on you? If your parents have ever moved from place to place during your time at home with them, what impact did the frequent moves have on you?

CONFLICT RESOLUTION	Providing tools for conflict resolution
	    Would say that your parents have provided you useful tools to resolve conflicts in your family?
	    Do you maintain respect when you seek to resolve a conflict?
	    Have you ever learned the art of constructive confrontation?

TRADITIONING	When prepare to pass on traditions
	    Are there stories, rituals, and customs you observed that have been generational in your family?
	    Do you do special activities for the holidays as well as the ordinary days that help teach children what your **family** values?
	    How have your family traditions been transformed?

TEACHING	Examine the ways you teach life lessons
	    How self-conscious are you about the lessons that you seek to teach the generations to come?
	    Are you aware that everything that you do is a part of your lesson book?

	How is your guidance given? In cruel ways, or thoughtful ways?
CAREGIVING	Create a caring environment in the home 　How is caring expressed in the family? 　Is the environment hospitable? 　Do you consider kindness a tradition in your family?
PROTECTION	Giving protection in the home 　How is protection rendered in your family? 　Does it feel safe in your home? 　Is it over-protective?
PROVIDING	Understanding how to provide in the home 　How is provision made? 　Is there a spirit of generosity? 　Is there miserliness?
NURTURING	A nurturing environment at home 　Who provides nurture in the family? 　Is father nurturing alongside mother? 　Is there an extended family that helps to nurture?
RITUALS	Role of rituals in the home 　Do you understand the power of rituals? 　What are the rituals consistently practiced, in your home, that hold the family together?
VALUES	What you value is important 　What are the priority values in the family? How are relationships to be constructed?

	How is family time spent? What beliefs, attitudes, and ideas are acceptable?

RELIGION	Checking your religious practices in the home
	    Is there a place for religion in the family?
	    How does religion influence family formation and decisions?
	    Is religion discussed at the dining table?
	    How does religion impact sexuality and affection?
	    How does religion help with the understanding of health?
	    Is church attendance important?
	    Is religion in the family experienced as liberating or oppressive?

SPIRITUALITY	Checking your spiritual leadership in the home
	    What is the spiritual maturity of those who are leaders in the home?
	    Are the leaders of the home, just religious, or are they also spiritual?
	    Is there consistency in their spirituality?
	    Is their passion for prayer and the study of Scripture?

COMMUNICATION	Communication key to building a strong home environment
	    How is communication done in the home? Do people know how to converse – dialogue – debate - listen, ask, and answer questions, with respect?
	    What kind of language and words they use?

COURAGE	Check how you teach courage at home
	    Do our children see us as courageous or cowardly parents?
	    Do our children understand that one does not have to be a superhero to be courageous?
	    Do our children understand that courage can be seen in small as well as in big things?

COMMITMENT	Lasting commitment
	    How do you show commitment about the home?
	    Do you show that you can stand by your word?
	    Do you persist in a relationship when times are good and when times are bad?

EMPATHY	Your capacity to show empathy
	    How is your empathic quotient?
	    Do you as a parent have a big heart?
	    Are you compassionate?
	    Are you sensitive to the pain of others?
	    Are you willing to suffer with others?

JUSTICE	Model what justice means in your home
	    Do you make clear that you, as a parent, believe in equality, equity, and justice for all or do you nurture favoritism that produces resentment?
	    What do you as a parent see in others, are they things to be respected, or are they objects to be trampled on?

LOVE	Love in the family
	    Many argue that "Love is caught, not taught."
	    What are the unique ways in which your family

	express love?
	Are they warm and affectionate?
	Do they have clear boundaries in how they express love?
	Do they allow permissive love?
	Do they confuse love with violence?
LOYALTY	Demonstrate loyalty in your home
	How well do you understand loyalty?
	Do you find ways of "criticizing or "backstabbing," and undermining and betraying those with whom you live and serve?

The challenge for parents is that they need to think in the long term of how they want to see their children in the future. Do they want to train leaders or mere followers? It is said that at birth parents offer their children certain legacies, but whatever is offered must be followed by effective training to achieve the positive results that every good parent would seek. The influence of parents counts. The vision of parents is far-reaching. The modeling of parents extends. So, ask yourself as a parent, what legacies you I leaving behind? And do not think of material things that you might leave behind so much, as the quality of character you help to build, the courage you help to develop, the convicted soul you produce, the committed attitude you generate, the high ideals you implant, and the fear of God you inspire in those who would be future leaders.

God will do a lot to help you, but it is true for the parent who seeks to leave a legacy of leaders, as it is true in any realm, that "God helps those who help themselves." So, as you go through life, in everything you do, think legacy, for you might be making a leader.

What Dr. Dorothy Law Nolte has said, in her legendary poem, **"Children Learn What They Live,"** about the power of parenting, is irrefutable:

> If children live with criticism, they learn to condemn.
> If children live with hostility, they learn to fight.
> If children live with fear, they learn to be apprehensive.
> If children live with pity, they learn to feel sorry for themselves.
> If children live with ridicule, they learn to feel shy.
> If children live with jealousy, they learn to feel envy.
> If children live with shame, they learn to feel guilty.
> If children live with encouragement, they learn confidence.
> If children live with tolerance, they learn patience.
> If children live with praise, they learn appreciation.
> If children live with acceptance, they learn to love.
> If children live with approval, they learn to like themselves.
> If children live with recognition, they learn it is good to have a goal.
> If children live with sharing, they learn generosity.
> If children live with honesty, they learn truthfulness.
> If children live with fairness, they learn justice.

If children live with kindness and consideration, they learn respect.

If children live with security, they learn to have faith in themselves and those about them.

If children live with friendliness, they learn the world is a nice place in which to live.

Even the individual gifts that children claim to possess are in part, legacies from their parents:

- Their personalities: That which gives them their dispositions
- Their characters: That is the mental and moral qualities that are distinctive to them
- Their intellect: That is their intelligence or capacity for reasoning
- Their talents: That is their aptitude and abilities
- Their gifts: That is special God-given capacities
- Their blessings: The favors of God are profoundly affected by the influence(s) of parents. For example, when parents say they bless their children, parents must know that they cannot bless by themselves, but that they are agents or channels of blessings. Blessings come from God, and curses come from the devil. Therefore, when parents bless their children, they have made themselves agents of blessings. When parents curse their children, they are channels of the evil one.

It is most significant what God said of Abraham:

> For I know him, that he will command his children and his household after him, and they shall keep the way of the LORD, to do justice and judgment; that the LORD may bring upon Abraham that which he hath spoken of him. (Genesis 18:19 KJV, emphasis mine).

> For I have chosen him, that he may command his children and his household after him to keep the way of the LORD by doing righteousness and justice, so that the LORD may bring to Abraham what he has promised him." (Genesis 18:19 ESV, emphasis mine).

What trust? Who would trust you with their child/ren? God trusted Abraham. God trusted Abraham by covenanting with him that through him, all the families of the earth would be blessed (Genesis 12). He did not do it because Abraham was perfect, but because God is willing to use the weakest of humanity to fulfill a mighty purpose of training an upcoming generation to be leaders.

God has given parents the privilege and responsibility of birthing and rearing children who become adolescents, young adults, and adults. When parents give birth to a child, they need to understand that they bear tremendous responsibility for the kind of person that the child turns out to be.

There are more messed up leaders in the world than the world needs. Without wishing to cast blame, their legacies have been passed on from their parents. If what I have said seems like casting blame, let us check out three of the most renown biblical patriarchs in Jewish history:

1. Abraham: Ask him why the difference between Ishmael and Isaac? Ask him about the relationship between Sarah and Hagar? Ask him about the impact of his double lies about Sarah being his sister, instead of being his wife, on his son Isaac?
2. Isaac: Ask him why the difference between Jacob and Esau? Ask him what is meant by "Isaac loved Esau, because of the venison," and "Rebecca loved Jacob"? Ask him why on the visit to Gerar he called Rebecca, his sister?
3. Jacob: Ask him about the resentment that built up in his family because of his favoritism toward Joseph? The envy got so thick that the brothers sold Joseph into Egyptian slavery.

There is no getting away from the responsibility for the negative legacies we have named above, but this does not say that the three characters did not have a profound positive impact. Abraham had a positive influence on Isaac as he passed the covenant blessings to him. Isaac reopened the wells that Abraham left behind. He also repaired the altars that Abraham had built. Then Isaac passed the covenant blessings to Jacob, who gave it to his sons. And the legacy continues. When Joseph visited with his father Jacob in his waning years, Jacob's eyes were dim, but when Joseph presented his two sons, Manasseh, and Ephraim to him, instinctively Jacob crossed his hands and gave the leadership blessing to Ephraim. Joseph tried to correct him, but Jacob repeated his action, making it clear that the younger would be greater than the older. On the return to Canaan, the name of Ephraim was used to represent ten tribes while Manasseh was subsumed under two tribes (Cf. Genesis 48). Jacob spoke the legacy of leadership in the final blessing of all his sons. As they stood at his bedside, before he breathed his last, he gave his evaluation of their behavior and character, and prophesied on what would be their roles in the leadership of Israel would be (Genesis 49).

It must have been an awesome moment, but the lesson was clear that parents can live and speak a legacy of leadership on their children.

THE MAKING OF LEADERS FOR THE NEXT GENERATION

In a follow up discussion on the influence of parents in developing leaders, let me turn to a personal story. I recall the lasting impression that my parents had in the development of my siblings and I into very effective leaders. Although we always felt his affirmation, yet in the years before his death, Dad made it clear that he was proud of the leadership successes of his children. When we felt that his assertions about our successes were getting too much, we could only smile and close our conversations by saying, "Praise the Lord, for his mercies Dad." Yes, we were acknowledging that without the help of God, neither Dad nor Mom, or any of us would have succeeded thus far. Of course, this acknowledge of the divine does not diminish the admiration and appreciation for what our parents did to nurture and encourage us to be the leaders we have become. Given the fact that Dad and Mom have lived longer than many other parents, Mom died at 96 and Dad at nearly 105, we have had more time with them than most children; time to receive their evaluation and advice, even into our late adulthood. Their advice was timely and personal, and we did our best to show our appreciation for their input.

If this reflection seems weighted towards Dad, it is because since he was in his late eighties, he often quoted the final episode in Jacob's life recorded in Genesis 49. Dad said many times, "before my death, I would like to have all my children at my bedside, as Jacob did, to pronounce blessings on each of them." At times, we felt that Dad recited his desire comically, but consciously, because he knew it would create some anxiety for some of us. He knew that most, if not all, wanted to know how he would bless us or prophesy on us. Dad did not get the chance to say all of what Jacob said on that death bed, since he had a stroke five weeks before his death and was reduced to silence. Although all of us went to see him weeks before, we were not present around his bed together. Even though we went to see him, spoke to him, and held the hand that he could raise, he could not talk back to us. We believe however, that in his silence, he gave us the blessings that he saw fit for each before passing to his rest at the ripe age of almost 105 years.

In reflecting on his legacy, we his children, continue to use one word above all, LEADERSHIP. Dad gave Mom a lot of credit for what they were able to accomplish. The fond ways he spoke of her, one might often get the impression that she did it by herself. But the partnership between Dad and Mom lasted for 71 years. Therefore, no one needs to question the impact of their powerful influence us. Their collaborative effort was to make sure they taught us how to be successful leaders. When we were younger, we did not talk of it, maybe because of our modesty, or that we did not take particular note of it. However, that changed when my wife, June, was researching for our book, *Parental Legacy*. As she and I were preparing the manuscript, she said to me, "Did you take note that leadership was so powerful a heritage in your family?" Her insight came while she was interviewing one brother who was very ill, and now deceased. She realized that all ten siblings were in leadership roles in various church and community organizations, in the four different countries in which we were living at the time. The different countries included Great Britain, Canada, the United States, and Jamaica, our original home. Was there communication and collaboration between communities, churches, pastors and other administrators in the different countries when selections - elections and ordinations were taking place? No. Were the places in which our sisters reside particularly open to women being ordained as church elders? We cannot say so. But the conclusion is clear that our parents were respected and effective leaders in our home, church, and community where we spent our formative years. Our parents later migrated to the England and Canada, respectively, and were respected strong as leaders in those communities where they resided

Not only were parents respected as leaders, but they were also seen as tremendous mentors, counselors, inspirers, advisers, and other great qualities that stood out in the circles of their influence. Local political leaders made efforts to recruit them in the political arena, but they knew that was not the path for them. When the pressure was overwhelming from the political leaders, Dad resigned his appointment as a local party group leader, because he felt it was crossing his effectiveness in the home and church. Spiritual leadership in the home, and the development of their children were more important to Mom and Dad than anything else. It was their belief that leadership begins in the home, and they took time to foster the development in that area. They allowed each child to lead out in family worship and in other spheres. Our teachers in the schools must have noticed something special about our potentials to lead because they were always calling on the different ones of us to lead in our classes. Some of us became school monitors, and others were called upon to lead out in plays and other activities that were intended to inspire other students how to lead.

Dad and Mom led by example. Whenever they had to perform any task in the church or community, we could see them diligently preparing for their presentation. They read and researched the journals and books that were available to them. They carefully wrote out their presentations, making clear their commitment to excellence, not only for themselves, but also to us as children. If we had to recite a Bible verse or poem or sing a song in church, our parents made sure that we rehearsed well, and presented to them before we could do so at church. If we were not ready in the evening, we had to make sure we were prepared by the morning of the presentation or we would have to reschedule for a future date. We did not like to reschedule, so we tried to be always prepared. We could not do anything sloppily. Dad and Mon did not hide their ambition about the building of leaders. Whenever our performance was acceptable, the community people cheered us on. Dad and Mom did not react in an arrogant way, for they seem to understand the impact their attitude could have on us. But we could sense their satisfaction with community affirmation we were receiving. However, they made sure that we understood that the highest praise belonged to God who gave us the ability to perform. They always repeated this quote from their favorite author, Ellen White, that the youth are to be trained "to be thinkers and not mere reflectors of other men's thoughts."

Dad and Mom knew how crucial it was for each child to have duties to perform, and they made sure that we knew their view on the importance of hard work. Each child had home duties, and we were never unaware of the importance of finishing what we started and doing it to the best of our abilities. Mom and Dad affirmed us when we did well, but at the same time, they corrected us when it was necessary. They were not afraid to give their disapproval. From them, it was all about training us to become the very best at what we had to do, be it great or small.

In spite of the fact that Mom and Dad were not financially stable, they had strong desires for the educational pursuits of each child . They made every effort for each child to live up to his/her potentials. In order to help each child in their academic development Dad and Mom made risky moves with the first and second child. They sent them away from home one at 15 and the other at 13 to the places they thought would give them access to the best high school education. Of course, on reflection, the decisions did not work out as was intended. However, the seed for each child to be fully educated was implanted early. And while Mom and Dad did not have the money to put us through college, they built the foundation and helped us to develop excellent reading skills. We got our head start schooling in family worship where we had to read aloud from the study quarterly, the devotional guide, and recite Bible texts we memorized during the week. Dad, in particular, taught us by example. He was an avid reader, reading books, journals, newspapers, or whatever substantive materials he could find. The diverse nature of his reading materials was way beyond his grade nine level of schooling. Anyone who visited our home in the early years, could not overlook Dad's little bookcase displaying his books. In it were books by authors such as, Dale Carnagie's (1936), *How to win friends and Influence People*; Richard C. Borden's (1935), *Public Speaking as Listeners Like It*; The life story of George Washington Carver, The Peanut Man; Frank Loris Peterson's (1934), The Hope of the Race; Hubert Swartout's (1943) *Modern Medical Counselor*: A Practical Guide to Health; and the compendium of Ellen White's writings including compilations, such as *Adventist Home; Counsel to Parents, Teachers and Students*, and *Child Guidance*. Dad was a Literature Evangelist, (colporteur or seller of religious books) for seven years, and in later years, he often spoke of the great opportunity it offered him to develop his ability to meet and interact with people of various backgrounds.

On his return to Jamaica, after residing in Canada for over 30 years, Dad built a house and made sure that he included a study which he also called his prayer room. The study had quite an assortment of books. Some he brought with from his Canada and many that he acquired, locally in Jamaica. Seeing the many volumes displayed in his library, many individuals could wonder if he read them or were they for show. Until three weeks before his stroke, Dad would head to his study/prayer room, on a daily basis. He sat for hours reading, writing and praying. Upon his death, the daughters who were searching the study were amazed to find many pieces of paper, notebooks and scratch pads that he used to make take note of the thoughts that impressed him from the various books on the shelves. The organization of ideas and themes he reflected on in the notes are profoundly impressive. The Francis Bacon says, " Says reading maketh a full man," and that really spoke of Dad. Reading shaped him and made him much of who he was.

Frankly, it was not what our Dad or Mom said so much that made us into leaders, but what they did. They created, at home, a climate and culture of leadership that focused on hardship and service. Intended or unintended, they were building from the earliest periods of our lives, the kinds of leaders we need to be. They did, what our grandma, who lived with them for 25 years, used to say, in her own vernacular, "Yuh haf fi laan fi dance a yaad, befor' yuh dance abroad" (You have to learn to dance at home before you dance on the street). Our home was a leadership university. And although Mom and Dad were not formally trained in leadership principles, they read much and imitated people they considered great leaders.

Yes, in preparing us to be leaders, Dad and Mom insisted that we spoke "proper" English, meaning that we could not speak in the common vernacular (, patois, creole) around the home. I do not know how well we spoke the "proper" English, but from all I know, every sibling is considered to be an effective communicator. Mom and Dad also taught us how to be direct in speech by saying exactly what we mean. They encouraged healthy debates at the dinner table, which helped us to be respectful of each other's ideas even if we did not agree. They taught us the power of asking questions. For them, questioning was one of the best ways of learning and sharing information. One thing that stands out in my mind, is how much emphasis Dad and Mom placed on us being able to communicate with confidence. While people often remark about the giftedness of speech in the family, we wish they would know that behind the scene there was a lot of practice, especially with some of us, at least if I speak for myself.

Dad and Mom believed in "do as I say and do." This of course included how to dress. They dressed in the most dignified, modest and appropriate manner to suit each occasion. That does not mean they dressed up all the time, but however they dressed, they were models of dignity. They also insisted that each of us as siblings, represent our home in the way we dressed. Consequently, when we had to leave home, each had to go through an inspection drill , as is done in Adventure, Pathfinders or the Scout – hair checked, shoes checked, and clothing checked. I did not always like the inspection, especially if Mom, who was the inspector, said, "Why is your hair not combed?" She would get a comb and start working it through the hair at a quick pace, and sometimes it did hurt. On one occasion, after a thorough inspection, Mom noticed that I needed a new pair of school pants. Since I was a frugal child and I saved some money, I could purchase the pants from my savings. Since I was using some of my savings to purchase the pants, I decided to buy what I liked, and what my peers were wearing. I thought too, that being fashionable would impress the girls at school. However, on reaching home, I found that Mom thought otherwise. She told in no uncertain term, how unsuitable my choice was. At fourteen years old, I thought I knew best and tried to protest and justify my purchase; I had to go back to the store and exchange the pants. As I grew older, I came to understand Mom's reasoning, which, of course, might seem quite harsh to most children in our contemporary generation. But it is still true that first impressions can be lasting. Once some individuals have an impression of you, that image stays with them until that first impression is erased. I do not wish to write an extended essay about first impressions, but the emphasis is that while our parents were not perfect, they were consistent, intentional, and persistent. They had their defects, but they tried their best to bring out the best qualities in us to make us effective leaders.

In fact, after taking note of us ten children who are, and have been active leaders in different communities, we now look look at the third generation and find that of twenty-four grandchildren, no less than twenty-two are fulfilling roles as influential leaders in their spheres of life. Some are performing beyond the wildest expectations And some have surpassed their parents in remarkable ways. Have they met all the expectations? To those who have set the highest bars, the answers might be a resounding, **No.** But in the common rung of what society is producing today, it is a good cycle in leadership. "The chips have not fallen far from the old blocks." That is why we are most thankful for the setting of the foundational blocks. Dad and Mom have been more effective than they could have dreamed. They credit their dedication to God and the tight-knit they had with many great community leaders. There were many pastors and their wives and many community leaders who gave support to our parents, but Mom and Dad were our number one mentors for most of what we learned in leadership.

Since Mom passed away seven years before Dad, we have had a longer time to evaluate Dad's legacy. I have been asking my siblings what each has noted about Dad that reflected his interest in his legacy of leadership. And it is of interest what each one observed. Here are ten things that they note about Dad.

1. He was a man of great courage – He was not afraid to stand up for what he believed is right, even if others might not like agree. Dad never displayed himself as a superhero, but he did many heroic things.
2. He was very committed to particular rituals that he used to enrich his life. He held as sacred his times of worship, his reading time which he called feeding his brain, and his sleep time. Dad liked to say, "Early to bed, early to rise, make a man healthy, wealthy and wise." He never became wealthy, but for the little he had at birth, one might say he came to the end of his life with a lot.
3. He was profoundly gentle, sensitive and compassionate. As he grew older, we noticed that these qualities seemed more evident. He grew more cool, calm and collective.
4. He knew how to let go of being "the boss" – As Dad came to his later years, he seemed to focus much more beyond the moment, in order "to pass the baton." He studied each child's personality and potential and decided on what responsibility he wanted each to have upon his death.
5. He always wanted to maintain his independence – Dad despised being dependent on others. He always found reasons to take a taxi to the nearest town. He delayed using a cane for

as long as he could. He sought to carry such independence to his grave, by making sure that he would set aside enough to cover his funeral expenses. He always said, "I do not want to be a burden to my children."

6. He was vulnerable in relationships – One of my brother's said that Dad had been rather stoic in his youthful days, but as he got older, he became more vulnerable to many with whom he might otherwise not take into his sphere. He always sought friends who could engage in serious intellectual discourse.

7. He was very contemplative and meditative – Although he was always prayerful, reflective and studious, yet as he had more time, he was more focused in these areas. While he would call the room in which he spent his reading time, his study, those who stayed in the home called it, Dad's prayer room.

8. He was focused on passing on the Jacob blessings to his children – Here is one thing with which Dad was so preoccupied that we wonder what he might have done if we were all gathered around his death bed and had the chance to speak. Our conviction is that he has already left us the blessings that he was capable of sharing.

9. He did not like to spend a long time with people who were not able to enter into in-depth or philosophical discussions. In this, he was very selective about his friends, and seemed delighted when University professors and students would stop by to dialogue and share his knowledge and wisdom.

10. He did not trust his memory. Posthumously, we got to find out that Dad seemed to write down everything. We found

notes on conversations that he wished to have with his children, outlines of short speeches, a diary with the names of his grand-children, their spouses and children, a record of funds he received and funds he sought to hide away.

11. He was a spiritual leader. If the faith tradition is very strong in the family, we credit it to Dad and Mom, who were consistent in family worship, church attendance, the study of God's word, and their daily walk with God about their home. During Mom's seven years of sickness and the seven years that Dad was alive after her death, the spiritual rituals continued very strongly in the home. Dad was very serious about his relationship with God and was ever determined to make clear where he stood on matters of faith.

12. He was very confidential - A grandfather one can trust. I have heard it from many persons how much they liked to speak with Dad, because what they shared with him would go to the grave with him. He was a secret keeper. One of our (my wife and I) son was dealing with a situation that we felt was not good for him. We were talking to him a lot, but felt we were not getting through to convince him of our wisdom. My wife and I spoke together and then we said, "son, why don't you write grandpa and hear what he has to say about it." From that day we felt sure that whatever grandpa said we did not need to know. We never asked our son what grandpa said, nor did we ask grandpa what our son had said. We were confident that whatever grandpa said, would be heavenly wisdom. Soon after our son's interaction with grandpa we saw the positive

difference. That son of ours is today an ordained church elder. Grandpa is silenced in death with the secret, but his legacy lives on in that son, as in others of grandpa's grandchildren. Dad did what he needed to do with our son, his grandson.

13. He was a visionary. Dad always liked to talk of the time when, before they were married, he and Mom sat on a rock, carved and shared the vision he had for the family. He always said, "The reason I marry her was because she shared my vision. And we prayed together."

14. He was legacy driven – When he was to celebrate his 100th birthday, we spoke with Dad about the legacy he wished to leave behind. He talked about the way he wanted to build a new generation of leaders by supporting their education. This is the basis of the Robert and Mary Kennedy Scholarship Fund, which is directed to students attending Northern Caribbean University. Several students have benefited already, but it was Dad's wish that upon his death the work would continue.

So much more to say about Dad, but we can cut to the chase with the words of Henry Wadsworth Longfellow said of great men in his Psalm of Life, poem:

> Lives of great men all remind us
> We can make our lives sublime,
> And, departing, leave behind us
> Footprints on the sands of time;

Footprints, that perhaps another,
Sailing o'er life's solemn main,
A forlorn and shipwrecked brother,
Seeing, shall take heart again.

Let us, then, be up and doing,
With a heart for any fate;
Still achieving, still pursuing,
Learn to labor and to wait

There is no question that leadership development in our home and family can be replicated in quite many homes and families. I do not wish to paint our picture rosier than others, but I speak of what I know best. And for all the tragic things that could have happened to us, I argue that there is some uniqueness about our legacy. After writing what I have, I sent it to my siblings and asked them what they thought. And here are some of their responses:

Marlow: I'm grateful that you have taken the time to compile these memorable moments that Mom and Dad have contributed to the foundation on which we now stand. As Frank has rightly said, many challenges existed for some, more than others, but through it, all God's hand still leads through the generations.

I do remember how important it was to rehearse before any presentation. I did not understand the significance then, but the seedling sowed, took root, grew into a tree (maybe not significant), but others can be sheltered now from those branches.

My shy, reserved, self, did not see leadership as one of my qualities, but on the job, in the community, at church, somehow, I have been often chosen to be the spokesperson for groups and sessions.

I thank God for parents who were committed to raising their family in the fear and admonition of the Lord.

Sonia: Mom and Dad gave us the foundational skills, and our early participation in church activities strengthened them. Recently, I was reflecting on the fact that I was elected to lead out in all the major ministries of the churches I have attended over the years. The exception being treasury. I never did much with finance, but I have assisted as a treasurer, unofficially. I am thinking, that apart from pushing faithfulness in tithe and offerings, Mom and Dad did not push being a treasurer much. I am not counting the stars in my crown; I am just reflecting on the great journey in leadership. Thank God for those early years, separated as we were, they molded and fashioned the legacies that bring meaning to our lives and the lives of others.

Eveythe: Parental legacy drives our society. That is why I thank God for praying, teaching, dedicated parents who guided us. As mentioned by others, sometimes I wonder how I find myself in church and school leadership. Often enough, I feel so inadequate, and I think that others are more competent than I am. But I look back and thank God for parents who gave us the needed training. Now that my children are grown, I hear them quoting and utilizing the same training tactics that we used in their upbringing. Praise God for the legacy given to us by God-fearing parents. Only eternity will reveal the tremendous legacy that we were bequeathed.

Frank: I read the inspirational lines and must confess that I did not feel like a leader at any time on the spectrum of things. While I took part in church and carried roles that were appreciated by others, I never thought of myself as a leader. In fact, I did not see myself even a good follower. In reflection on my career path, it was others who talked much about my leadership qualities. I do not know how deliberate Dad and Mom were in structuring the leadership path, but it appears to me that their quest was for all to do their best and they took the initiative in demonstrating what leadership should look like. Despite all of the contrary paths in my life, God helped me to find a way in what He wanted me to be. I have been able to rely on much of the early examples in a particular way to answer the call. It has not been easy, but at moments of deep reflection, and in the career path and practice, I have much to praise God about. I have seen too many children with the greatest of potential ended up on "the scrap heap."

If the struggle with the care of sheep, goats, rabbits, chickens, collecting firewood, drawing water from the cistern, running errands, plus the cuts, and bruises along the way have anything to do with leadership and serving others, then we cannot discount that those moments around Dad and Mom were highly valuable. Also, the presentation skills we learned helped to make our experiential leadership possible. Greatest of all, what we learned about understanding the human condition was nothing less than what we could have gotten through university education. Indeed, such seems to be a hallmark of the family.

Nylann: Dad believed in excellence. Period. It seems to be a point of emphasis in all his children. The claim might be quite biased and arrogant, some might say. But it is true, we do believe in excellence.

In summation

Our mother passed away just after her 96th birthday, but her legacy lives on. Our father reached the ripe old age of nearly 105, and it was quite amazing to watch him in his daily routine, how much he carried from his earliest days into his latter days. At the break of day, when he arose, he entered his study and read, meditated and prayed for about 45 minutes. At about 7:00 AM, he would call any member of the family present in the house to the family/worship room. It is incredible that even to the last six weeks before his death, how much he would take charge. Our sister, who cared for him, took note of his leadership style and would call him an "Alpha male." He would tell her what song he wished for the morning. He would decide on the devotional reading of the day and then decide on who would do the prayer. A few times he would ask this sister/daughter for a selection, but whenever one of his sons came around, our sister says, Dad would differ, by saying, "son, you lead." Although I might have overstated Dad's actions in the leadership of worship, as told by our sister, the point I make is that Dad, at nearly 105, was still the chief in his house. He was a leader, *par excellence*.

The point of the multiple areas of reflection on Dad and Mom is to give a glimpse into the backdrop that influenced one home and family on the legacy of leadership. The story is not for boast, but to show that what happens in one home and family is replicable in any family. One family of leaders make many generations of leaders. Leadership development begins in the home. In biblical understanding, there needs to be a clear focus on the future generation, so that as one generation pass to another generation there will be continuity and stability. This does not say that one might not have variations in which persons might not have strong parental models or family support and yet develop the skills to become influential leaders. But it seems incontestable that the most effective leaders are from homes and families where parents model good leadership.

Passing the mantle of leadership to the next generation is what brings leadership success. That means, if we are to see a society in which there are more effective leaders, we need to find parents who will accept their responsibility for training such leaders. Yes, leadership begins at home. It starts in the womb. It is nurtured in the breast, in the nest, and will find its manifestations in varied contexts of society. We need to be concerned about the loss of leadership influence in the home, for as the home goes so goes the society.

CONCLUSION

Each one of us has been given a sphere of influence. How lasting the impact we have on our sphere has been the concerns of our reflections. Some people's power has been short-lived, while others persist through generations. One of the things that we need to remind ourselves of more often than we like to is that we are never in our circle of influence, forever. Soon someone comes along to take our place. Unfortunately, not many persons take the time to reflect on their temporality in their circle of influence. If everyone did, we would be more conscious as to how we act in the sphere of influence and the legacy that we are leaving behind.

The failure to understand the power of influence is why the world is facing such a shortage of positively, effective leadership. There is a drought for such leadership in the political and public spheres today. Of course, such a drought is also well expressed in the private areas such as our homes, where fathers and mothers have lost their influence upon their children and in churches where the sense of authority is disrespected. Yes, in many spheres, the legacy of leadership is missing.

It is my trust, then, that as one reads through this collection of opinion editorials and sermonic notes, that such a one will be motivated to focus on the legacy in their sphere of influence. All of us need to think more of what legacies we are bequeathing to the next generation. We need to understand that somebody is always within the circle of our influence.

If you have not checked concerning your circle of influence lately, you might want to reread my reflections and take a leadership legacy assessment test. There are many assessment tests from which to select, but I recommend one from www.Coursehero.com. It might not be too late to make sure that you leave the most lasting legacy for those who will follow in your train.

APPENDIX

ASSESSING YOUR LEGACY OF LEADERSHIP

Every person who leads should assess themselves, to see what kind of legacy they wish leave. It is impossible to lead and not leave a legacy. Test yourself to see the impact of your legacy. The table below is intended to help in the process of your self-assessment. Respond on a scale of 0-4 to each question or suggestion. 0=Never 1=Seldom 2=Sometimes 3= Usually 4=Always

Assessment questions or suggestions	0 Never	1 Seldom	2 Sometimes	3 Usually	4 Always
I have a clear understanding of the direction in which I need to move with my life and the organization I lead.					
I take time to share what I understand concerning the vision of my life and the organization/institution I lead					
I do all I can to motivate others to work alongside me.					
I trust in people to develop their competence.					
I am very effective with					

the proper distribution of the resources in the organization I work or lead.					
I have great respect for other people's ideas and opinions.					
I lead by setting a positive example that inspires others.					
I am very effective at coaching and developing people.					
I take time to identify and encourage the development of the potential of the people who are around me.					
When I am to work with others, I find ways of fostering a team-spirit.					
Harboring resentment towards others has weakened my authority in leadership.					
When I face challenges in leadership my first reaction is to run away.					
When I am in a hard spot, I find it easy to					

withdraw from the public view.					
I have certain core values that I will not negotiate.					
I find it very easy to fight back when people attack me.					
When I am in a leading position, I take time to build cooperative relationships.					
When I delegate to people and they are not prompt in doing what needs to be done, I do it myself.					
I work effectively with others who are different from me.					
I understand that leadership demands a spirit of self-sacrifice.					
I leverage networks of people to resource and strengthen my leadership.					
I keep others informed about what I'm doing, wherever it affects them.					

I am very open about building up others.					
I follow through on the promises and commitments that I make.					
I am open to making significant changes in my behavior when necessary.					
I am able to exert self-discipline when needed.					
I feel comfortable when those I lead share their pain with me.					
I have a strong sense of justice that is directed by empathy.					
I am driven by great passion in the things I do?					
Do you act as the go between when others are in conflict around you?					
Are you known to be relentless when pursuing initiatives?					
I am open to suggestions from my					

colleagues and subordinates?					
Are you regarded as methodical when you have a task to accomplish?					
I encourage initiative and innovation?					
When people come to me with complaints, I take time to listen.					
When I have to make a decision, I take time to call out all the facts.					
I make tough decisions regardless of people's approval or rejection.					
To garner diverse perspectives, I solicit input from my team members.					
I have a game plan for personal growth					
I respond to change in a positive way					
I believe in honesty and transparency in all aspects of my leadership.					
I understand the ethical responsibility that comes with					

leadership and act accordingly.					
I challenge others to make right choices in whatever they do.					
I am effective in defining and clarifying priorities in my life and organization					

After scanning your answers on the grid above, write a short sentence on how you feel about your leadership capacity, skills, style, development and legacy. What are some areas that show the need for growth and what needs radical transformation? Have you been honest with yourself?

_____
_____
_____
_____
_____

CONNECTING WITH US

If you wish to receive education on any issue in our Legacy Seminars series:

- Parental Legacy
- Parental Advocacy
- Life Maps Legacy
- The Legacy of Love
- Legacy Minded Men,
- The Legacy of Leadership

Contact us by email: legacyseminars41@gmail.com;
Phone: 862-224-1097

www.ingramcontent.com/pod-product-compliance
Lightning Source LLC
LaVergne TN
LVHW041541070426
835507LV00011B/870